LIVING Our FAITH
Church
A Community of Faith

CHAPTER 1

The People of the Old Testament

God, maker of time and eternity, you are the true author of history. Teach us to see your loving action in the stories of Scripture. Guide us on our journey, you who are without beginning and end. Amen.

LIVING Our FAITH

Church
A Community of Faith

Principal **Consultants**

Dennis J. Bozanich, MBA

Michael Carotta, EdD

Rev. Leonard Wenke, MDiv

Principal **Reviewers**

Mary Lee Becker, MPM

Robert J. Kealey, EdD

M. Annette Mandley-Turner, MS

Harcourt
Religion Publishers

Nihil Obstat
Rev. Richard L. Schaefer
Censor Deputatus

Imprimatur
✠ Most Rev. Jerome Hanus, OSB
Archbishop of Dubuque
January 31, 2001
Feast of Saint John Bosco, Patron of Youth and Catholic Publishers

The nihil obstat and imprimatur are official declarations that a book or pamphlet is free of doctrinal or moral error. No implication is contained herein that those who granted the nihil obstat and imprimatur agree with the contents, opinions, or statements expressed.

Our Mission
The primary mission of Harcourt Religion Publishers is to provide the Catholic and Christian educational markets with the highest quality catechetical print and media resources. The content of these resources reflects the best insights of current theology, methodology, and pedagogical research. These resources are practical and easy to use, designed to meet expressed market needs, and written to reflect the teachings of the Catholic Church.

Photography Credits
Art Resource: Erich Lessing: 48; Scala: 27; **Bridgeman Art Library:** Fitzwilliam Museum, University of Cambridge, UK: 18; Galleria dell'Accademia, Florence, Italy: 54; Musee Rodin, Paris, France/Peter Willi: 88; Museo dell'Opera del Duomo, Florence, Italy: 56; Ary Scheffer, Louvre, Paris: 68; **Catholic Relief Services:** 75; **Christie's Images:** 7; Superstock: 20; **The Crosiers:** Gene Plaisted: 14, 19, 46, 48, 59, 66, 86, 99; **Corbis:** Vittoriano Rastelli: 67; **Digital Imaging Group:** Erik Snowbeck: 17; **Dominicans, St. Vincent Ferrer Priory:** Gary Stolberg: 97; **FPG International:** Marco Corsetti: 67; Kevin Laubacher: 70; Miguel S. Salmeron: 4; Sanderling: 37; Telegraph Colour Library: 5; VCG: 4; **Robert Cushman Hayes:** 103; **Jack Holtel:** 4, 6, 8, 16, 26, 31, 34, 36, 41, 48, 49, 54, 66, 77; **Image Bank:** L. D. Gordon: 61; Eric Meola: 11; Maria Taglienti: 54; Charles West: 12; **Impact Visuals:** Thor Swift: 94; **Index Stock:** 4, 5, 44, 98; **Liaison International:** Fornaciari: 78; **Madonna House Archives,** Combermere, Ontario, Canada K0J1L0: 17; **Maryknoll Missioners:** Theisen: 98; **National Conference of Catholic Bishops:** 28; **Natural Bridges:** Robert Lentz: 54, **Nicholas Studios:** Nick Falzerano: 58; 87; **PhotoDisc, Inc.:** 76; **PhotoEdit:** Robert Brenner: 43; Michael Bridwell: 32; Myrleen Ferguson Cate: 59; Tony Freeman: 45; A. Ramey: 51; David Young-Wolff: 76, 91; **Photo Researchers:** George Holton: 66; Richard Nowitz: 92; **Jake Price:** 36; **Salesians of Saint John Bosco:** 97; **Skjold Photographs:** 83; Stock Boston: Bob Daemmrich: 15, 29; Najlah Feanny: 79; **Stock Market:** 28; Vivane Moos: 67; Jose L. Pelaez: 101; David Pollack: 80; Nancy Santullo: 54; **Stone:** Christopher Bissell: 74; Myrleen Ferguson Cate: 18; Howard Grey: 72; Louis Grandadam: 24; Earth Imaging: 66; Lori Adamski Peek: 47; Jake Rajs: 84; Don Smetzer: 54; Patrisha Thomson: 50; **Superstock:** The Cummer Museum of Art and Gardens, Jacksonville: 46; Kactus Foto, Santiago, Chile: 38; Diana Ong: 24; **Unicorn Stock:** Robin Rudd: 65; Aneal Vohra: 85; **Jim Whitmer Photography:** Jim Whitmer: 22, 28; **W. P. Wittman Photography:** Bill Wittman: 16

Cover Photos
Unicorn Stock: Robin Rudd; **Skjold Photographs**

Feature Icons
Catholics Believe: Jack Holtel; **Opening the Word:** PictureQuest; **Our Christian Journey:** PictureQuest: Chuck Fishman/Contact Press Images

Location and Props
Dayton Church Supply; St. Christopher Catholic School, Vandalia, OH; St. Peter Catholic School, Huber Heights, OH

Skills for Christian Living
The skill steps in Applying the Bible, and the Name It, Tame It, Claim It process, both from the *Catholic and Capable* series, are used with permission from Resources for Christian Living.

Printed in the United States of America

ISBN 0-15-900500-0

10   9   8   7   6

Read the reflection below and circle any phrases that answer the question for you.

With whom have you made promises and commitments that affect your life?

family   teachers   God   coaches

neighbors   friends   government officials

Consider how these people influence your life, and write down a few of the ways they support you day by day.

_____

_____

_____

_____

Promises

Your place within history is the result of a web of relationships that weave back through time. Your family history, the history of your country, and the history of the world are filled with stories of promises. Scripture, too, is filled with promises—promises made by God to his people, and promises made by the Israelites to God. God's promises, as we know, were always kept. Unfortunately, the promises of his people were sometimes broken.

We make promises every day—to our family, our friends, and even ourselves. But the most important promises we make are to God. Among other things we promise to honor him and trust in his guidance. When we keep our promises to God, we share in his love and grace. But when we break our promises to God, we distance or separate ourselves from him. Our role as members of his Church is to open ourselves to do his will, to recognize our part in the tradition of our faith.

Forming Good
Relationships

Relationships take time. If you have ever moved into a new neighborhood or transferred to a different school, you know how tough it can be to make new friends. Strangers become friends only in time and after a personal investment has been made on both sides. You have to spend time talking, sharing activities, and just "hanging out" together to learn about another person. You have to build trust, first in small ways and then in more important ways. And finally, you have to give something of yourself to the other person. As you reveal yourself to others, you can begin to know them and they can begin to know you. When we come to know another person, love becomes possible.

These statements about human relationships are just as true in our relationship with God. If God were completely unknowable, it would be impossible to have a relationship with him. But God chooses to enter into relationship with us and to reveal himself to us. This is known as **revelation.** God reveals himself and his love in the beauty of creation, in the events of salvation history, and most of all in Jesus. One of the most important ways God reveals himself is through the Bible. Because the Bible tells stories of God's faithfulness to his promises and his unending love and forgiveness, those stories continue beyond the pages of the Bible. The threads of God's story are woven into our lives.

Catholics Believe

God reveals himself to us so that we can respond to him, know him, and love him. See Catechism, #52.

Which of the ways God reveals himself helps you best know and respond to God at this time in your life? Explain your answer.

_____

_____

_____

How the
Story Is Told

The Bible has two sections: the Old Testament and the New Testament. Together they make up the word of God we call **Scripture,** which means "holy writing." The Old Testament starts at the very beginning of time with two stories of creation in the Book of Genesis. From the beginning God created the world filled with holiness and justice. But as a result of sin, men and women now face hardship and suffering, sickness and death. Yet even after *original sin* replaces the state of original blessing, God does not abandon humans. Our God, as the Old Testament often reminds us, saves us and wants to be in a loving relationship with us.

The story of God's saving actions is often called **salvation history.** Salvation history begins with creation, continues through the events recorded in Scripture, and will last until the end of time. Throughout human history God has acted in many ways to save us. Some of his ways are as large and complex as saving the human race through Noah's family. Others may be as small and simple as God assuring the stuttering Moses that Aaron could speak for him before Pharaoh. No saving act is too large or too small for God.

Read and reflect on the story of Noah. Share your thoughts with your Faith Partner.

Sacred
Promises

The saving acts recorded in Scripture go hand in hand with God's promises. One story in the Old Testament tells of a time when people chose to ignore God. Noah's family was saved from destruction by obeying God and building the ark. In return God promised Noah and his descendants never to destroy the world again with a flood. (See *Genesis 8–9.*) This sacred and binding promise or agreement between God and humanity is known as a **covenant.** The sign of the covenant between God and Noah is the rainbow.

The covenant continues to be revealed to us through God's relationship with Abraham. In the story of Abraham, God spoke to him and offered to lead him to a far-off promised land. God told Abraham that he and his wife, Sarah, would be blessed with a child even though they were beyond the age when couples normally conceive children. His faith was rewarded with the birth of Isaac. God told Abraham that his descendants would be as numerous as the stars in the sky or the grains of sand on the shore. (See *Genesis 22:17.*) It is from Isaac's son Jacob, who was given the name "Israel," that the Israelites took their name.

In Jacob's lifetime there was a famine in Canaan, and the Israelites moved to Egypt. Years later, after the Egyptians had enslaved the Israelites, God performed the greatest saving act in the Old Testament. The Book of Exodus tells the extraordinary story of how God led the Israelites out of slavery in Egypt. God spoke to the Israelites and to Pharaoh through Moses and Aaron. It was through Moses that God renewed his covenant in one of the best-known stories of the Old Testament. The Ten Commandments, contained within the Law of Moses, became the enduring sign of the Israelites' promise to live in relationship with God.

Our Christian Journey

A Brave Faith In 1980 four Catholic missionaries were murdered in El Salvador. Ita Ford and Maura Clarke were Maryknoll sisters. Dorothy Kazel belonged to the order of Ursuline sisters. Jean Donovan was a lay missionary from the Diocese of Cleveland, Ohio. All four women were motivated by a concern for, and offered their services to, people suffering from political oppression and poverty. Details of their deaths are unclear, but it is believed that their car was stopped by members of the El Salvadorian military who opposed their missionary work. The soldiers executed the four women and buried them in shallow graves on the side of the road. The cruel deaths of the four missionaries focused the world's attention on the troubled situation in El Salvador and the other countries in Central America. The faith of the people in El Salvador has been strengthened by the example of these women, and the people continue to trust in God's promise.

For further information: Read *The Same Fate as the Poor* by Judith Noone, *Salvador Witness: The Life and Calling of Jean Donovan* by Ana Carrigan, or watch the movies *Roses in December* or *Choices of the Heart*.

1975   2000

1978
JOHN PAUL II ELECTED POPE

1980–1988
RONALD REAGAN SERVES AS
PRESIDENT OF THE UNITED STATES

1980
BISHOP OSCAR ROMERO MARTYRED IN EL SALVADOR

1980
FOUR MISSIONARIES TO EL SALVADOR MARTYRED

Broken Promises

God is always faithful to his promises. But humans have often failed to keep their promises. The first five books of the Bible, known as the **Pentateuch** or Torah, reveal God's ongoing faithfulness to the covenant between himself and his people. By choosing disobedience over and over again, humans fail to keep their part of the covenant. Periodically throughout salvation history God sent prophets to *reconcile,* or reunite, the people with their Lord by calling them back to a right relationship with him. But the people often went astray by worshiping other gods, a practice known as *idolatry.*

Like the people of the Old Testament, we also tend to worship other things in our lives, such as money, clothes, music groups, and sports figures. Through it all God always calls us back to a relationship with him. And there is something within us that yearns for the peace and happiness that only friendship with God can give.

The books of prophecy and other writings of the Old Testament remind us how near God is at all times and how far sin removes us from experiencing his love. Salvation history traces the longing of all humans for God who promises to save us.

Focus On

The Pentateuch
The five biblical books of the Pentateuch contain the stories from creation to the death of Moses. These books, also known as the Books of the Law, or Torah, are *Genesis, Exodus, Leviticus, Numbers,* and *Deuteronomy.*

Opening the Word

Not with our ancestors did the LORD make this covenant, but with us, who are all of us here alive today.
Deuteronomy 5:3

Read *Deuteronomy 5* as well as *Genesis 15:1–21* and *1 Corinthians 11:23–26.* Name one promise that you think God has made with you.

_____

Keeping the Promise

When we hear the stories of the covenant from the Old Testament, it is easy to think of them as belonging to other people in the distant past. The stories of Noah, Abraham, and Moses were written thousands of years ago and were part of oral tradition for many generations before that. The God who made the covenant with humans is with us through the action of the Holy Spirit today. God's sacred promise remains unbroken. Christians believe that through Jesus, whose story is the center of the New Testament, the covenant is fulfilled for all people. Jesus' sacrifice, his suffering and death on the cross, is the ultimate example of how far God will go to embrace us. And Jesus' death and resurrection are the ultimate effective signs of reconciliation with God—for all people, for all time.

God's relationship with us is precious to him. It is the goal of all salvation history. What God wants most is for us to experience his eternal love. All he asks is that we say "yes," or "Amen."

Loved Throughout History

Although it sometimes feels as if we are all alone, none of us lives in isolation. From the moment our lives began, our relationship to the people and events surrounding us influenced our history. Through all of our experiences, we became who we are today. Our lives are stories of relationships—stories of promises kept and broken.

In the stories of creation, we learn that God made the world and offered people his love, but the first people rejected friendship with God and were unfaithful. By choosing sin, the first humans were responsible for the entrance of suffering and death into the world. The original holiness and justice God had given humans was lost to original sin.

But God loves us and wants to save us. And the story of his loving and saving actions continues today. When we feel abandoned by our friends, we can open ourselves to his presence and feel accepted and protected. If we have hurt someone by our words or actions—or if someone has hurt us—we can experience God's grace when we open ourselves to the reconciliation process. Each day God reveals himself to us in the people and events of our lives. Through our friends, family, and Church, God is present to us, supporting us and directing our way.

Reflect on which Old Testament event is meaningful to you and why. Share your thoughts with your Faith Partner.

FaiTH ParTNeRSHiP

WRAP UP

- **Our relationships, including our relationship with God, are interwoven with promises.**
- **Salvation history is the story of God's saving actions out of love for humanity.**
- **God continues to reveal his divine presence to us in creation, Scripture, salvation history, and most of all in Jesus.**
- **Jesus is the fullness of the revelation of God's love for us.**

What questions do you have about the information presented in the chapter?

_____

_____

_____

Around the Group

Discuss the following question as a group.

How can we mend relationships that have been hurt by broken promises?

After everyone has had a chance to share his or her responses, come up with a group answer upon which everyone can agree.

_____

_____

_____

What personal observations do you have about the group discussion and answer?

_____

_____

_____

Briefly. . .

At the beginning of this chapter, you were asked with whom you have made promises and commitments that affect your life. Now that you have learned more about promises and relationships, identify the promises in your life that make you who you are.

_____

_____

_____

Applying the
Bible Message

Expressions of Faith-

Reading God's message in Scripture can help us understand how we can live out his plan for us. By reading the Bible and applying its message to our lives, we can learn what it means to share God's love with others.

Scripture

Your word is a lamp to my feet and a light to my path.
Psalm 119:105

Think About It-

Based on the lessons you remember from Scripture, mark the following statements true or false:

_____ God created all life.

_____ It is better for me to tell the truth.

_____ Breaking a promise is no big deal.

_____ If somebody needs my help, I should offer it.

_____ Sometimes it is okay to steal.

_____ God doesn't care about me.

Skill Steps

Learning about Scripture is not just about remembering the words. It is also learning how to apply God's message to our lives. The Scriptures speak to us in many ways about our
Conscience—what is right and what is wrong.
Character—the kind of people we are.
Contribution—what we do to help others.
Knowledge of God—the nature and characteristics of God.

Any time you hear or read the word of God, ask yourself this question: *Is God's word speaking to me about my conscience, character, contribution, or knowledge of God?* Your answer will make it much easier to know how to apply God's word to your life.

Look up the following passages in the Old Testament, and match them with the four areas of your life.

_____ *Deuteronomy 5:17–19*   **a.** Conscience

_____ *Deuteronomy 15:7–8*   **b.** Character

_____ *Job 12:8–10*   **c.** Contribution

_____ *Proverbs 16:32*   **d.** Knowledge of God

Check It Out

Place a check mark next to the following statements that pertain to you:

◯ I read the Bible often.

◯ I believe the Bible has a lot to say to me today.

◯ The Bible has been an important part of the way I live my life.

◯ My family places importance on the Bible.

◯ I wish I knew more about the Bible.

Based on your responses, how might you increase the importance of the Bible in your life?

_____

_____

Closing Prayer

O God, our Creator, you made us, and you promised to be with us always through the power of the Holy Spirit. Through Jesus you kept your promise and showed us the greatness of your love. Help us always believe in your word and follow your direction by doing good and caring for others as you care for us. Amen.

The Early Church

Jesus, by sharing our human life and death, you show us the love of the Father. Teach us through the good news of the gospel to live as your brothers and sisters. Lead us into everlasting life. Amen.

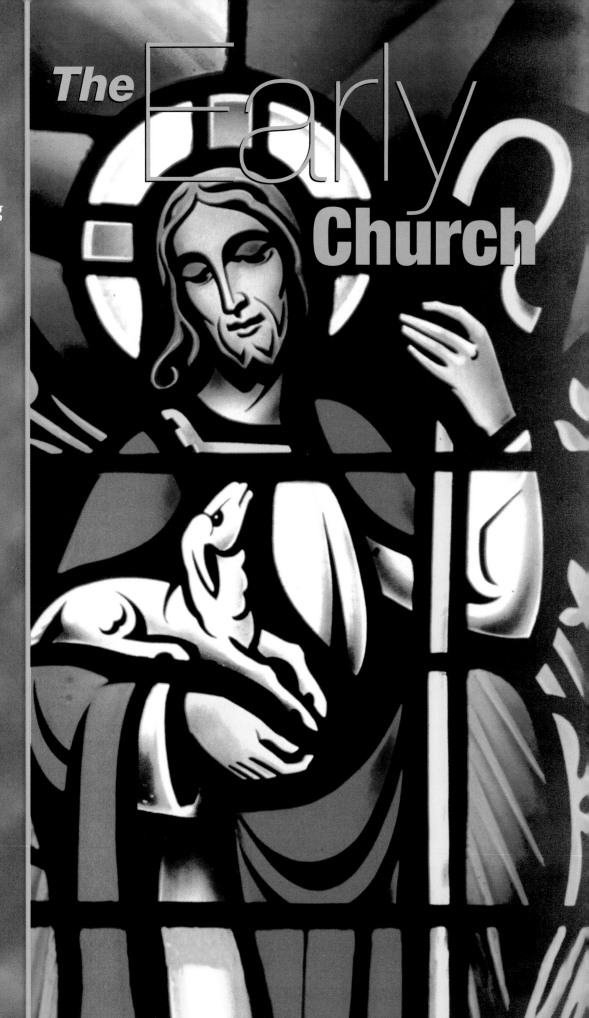

Name a person or a few people who have influenced your values the most.

_____

_____

_____

_____

What about these people has encouraged you to follow their actions or advice?

_____

_____

_____

_____

Follow the Leader

Those who become our leaders usually have certain qualities that make them stand out. Some people lead by their intelligence or because they are in positions of authority. Others lead by the natural magnetism we call *charisma* or because they have acquired power and influence. Still others lead by example. We trust leaders whom we respect because of their values and their character. Choosing whom to follow is a serious responsibility.

By making wise decisions as followers, we become like the leaders we choose. If we choose to follow good leaders, we can learn from them and become effective leaders ourselves.

Almost two thousand years ago, a small group of people became followers of a teacher from Galilee. The decision to follow Jesus changed their lives and the lives of many other people forever. This story becomes the story of the Church.

Waiting for a Leader

What qualities make a good leader? Physical strength, beauty, or charisma are often the attributes that pass for leadership. But it is important to look for more meaningful and long-lasting qualities from those whom we choose to follow.

Scripture is filled with stories of leaders. Some were successful, and some were not. Many of the best leaders were also the most unlikely. David was still a young boy when God sent Samuel to anoint him king of Israel. Isaiah called himself unworthy to speak for God. Unexpectedly, Deborah, a prophet and a judge, led her people to victory over their enemies. God chooses men and women who are young or old, worthy or unworthy, ready or reluctant.

Throughout the events recorded in the Old Testament, God chose many leaders. Some leaders, such as Joshua, led the people into battle. Some, like Isaiah, called the people back to the covenant. And some, such as Ezra, interpreted God's laws. No matter what kind of leader God chose, each of them had to deal with people who sometimes were stubborn and refused to follow.

The covenant God forged with the Israelites was renewed in the time of King David, but at this time the people struggled to live God's law. The famous temple in Jerusalem, built by David's son, Solomon, to house the Ark of the Covenant, did little to make the people more faithful. After Solomon's death the kingdom was fragmented by power struggles. Remembering David, the people longed for a new leader—a *messiah,* or anointed one—to unite them and guide them.

Opening the Word

5th Sunday of Lent, Cycle B

But this is the covenant that I will make with the house of Israel after those days, says the LORD: I will put my law within them, and I will write it on their hearts; and I will be their God, and they shall be my people. Jeremiah 31:33

Read *Jeremiah 31:31–34* as well as *Romans 2:15–16, 1 Corinthians 12:27–31,* and *2 Corinthians 3:2–3.* How would a law written on people's hearts be different from a law imposed on them by someone else?

_____

_____

The New Covenant

In the time of the Old Testament, the covenant was made between God and the Israelites. Then God sent his Son as the new covenant, which is for all people.

Think for a moment of the manger scene at Christmas. Invisible but central to this joyful scene is the deep love of our God, who enters into human history to save us at any cost. What appears to be a private scene actually means much more. Jesus, the son born to Mary, is also the Son of God. The title **Christ,** which we use as a name for Jesus, means "anointed one," or *messiah.* With the birth of Jesus, the **gospel,** the good news of God's saving love, begins.

The New Testament contains four books called the *Gospels* that tell us about Jesus' life and teachings. The Gospels of Matthew, Mark, Luke, and John were written by disciples of Jesus in the first generations after his death. A **disciple** is one who accepts and spreads the teachings of another. Many disciples surrounded Jesus during his life, and some became the leaders of the early Church. Mary, the mother of Jesus, is recognized as the first disciple.

OUR CHRISTIAN JOURNEY

A New Disciple

Catherine de Hueck Doherty has been described as "a woman in love with God." Born in Russia and raised in the Russian Orthodox Church, she later became Catholic. While living in Canada in the 1930s, Catherine acted on her passion for the gospel and began Friendship House, a Catholic interracial mission. She saw the need to support equality and mutual respect among people of different races, creeds, social classes, cultures, and genders. Friendship House became a place where people could meet and reach beyond their differences. Later, she also founded Madonna House, a gathering place for a group of lay men and women and priests whose lives are committed to living Jesus' teachings.

For more information: Research Friendship House **(www.friendshiphouse.org)** or Madonna House **(www.madonnahouse.org)** on the Internet or ask a librarian to help you find a copy of *Poustinia,* by Catherine de Hueck Doherty.

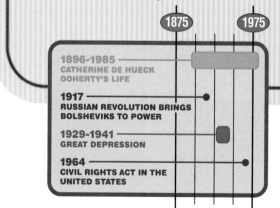

1875   1975

1896-1985
CATHERINE DE HUECK DOHERTY'S LIFE

1917
RUSSIAN REVOLUTION BRINGS BOLSHEVIKS TO POWER

1929-1941
GREAT DEPRESSION

1964
CIVIL RIGHTS ACT IN THE UNITED STATES

Renewing the Covenant

The Eucharist we celebrate at Mass is the "new and everlasting covenant" between God and those who put their faith in Jesus Christ.

Answering the **Call**

Have you ever felt an inner sense of urgency to change your life? Have you ever met someone so impressive that you wanted to **become just like that person**, even if it meant leaving old ways and relationships behind?

Many people in the time of Jesus heard the call to change their lives. Jesus called fishermen away from their nets in Galilee and a tax collector away from his accounts. When those who were poor heard the good news, many of them followed Jesus to hear more. Some whom he healed of illnesses also remained with him. When Jesus offered forgiveness to those bound by sin, they, too, wished to stay with him. To these people, Jesus was offering words of life.

The twelve **apostles** who followed Jesus shared a special closeness to him. The word *apostle* means "one who is sent." The number twelve was important because it stood for completeness and corresponded to the twelve tribes of Israel in the Old Testament. Christians see in Jesus' selection of twelve apostles a connection with the Israelite tradition.

A New Kind of **Leader**

Jesus was a charismatic leader with great integrity because he lived what he taught. Though he used **parables,** stories used to teach, to preach about God's kingdom, he also shared his good news through his actions. He fed those who were hungry, gave sight to those who were blind, and renewed the strength of those who were disabled. Those trapped in their sins were freed by forgiveness. And when Jesus raised the dead, as in the story of Lazarus, many people came to believe that this man was truly anointed by God.

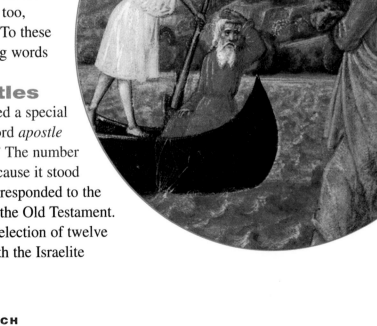

Sent Out to All the World

When we hear that something exciting is going to happen, we rush to tell everyone we know. The good news of the early Church was like that. Into a world filled with sin, suffering, and death, Jesus introduced new life in the reign of God. When Easter dawned and Jesus rose from the dead, a new era of salvation history opened. Sin and everlasting death lost their power over us.

Before Jesus returned to his Father, he gave the apostles the mission of proclaiming the good news to the whole world. On the Jewish feast of Pentecost, the Holy Spirit, in a form like wind and fire, came to the room where the disciples had gathered. Blessed with the gifts of the Holy Spirit, they rushed into the streets of Jerusalem to preach the gospel. The Church began to grow from that hour, and through this Church—the Body of Christ—Jesus continues his saving mission to this day.

As members of this same Church, we share the mission given to the apostles. Jesus promised to be with his Church until the end of time, and we celebrate his presence in the covenant of his Body and Blood at every Eucharist. We share in the life of the Church as the new disciples of Jesus. We proclaim the good news of salvation to a new generation.

Catholics Believe

Christianity is the religion of the "Word" of God, not written, but incarnate (made flesh, or human) and alive. See Catechism, #108.

What signs do you see that Christianity is alive today?

_____

_____

_____

Share your thoughts with your Faith Partner. FaiTH PaRTNeRSHiP

God Leads Us to Life

Whether we are at school, at church, out with friends, or on the playing field, the leaders among us help determine how things will go. Maybe you're a leader in your group, or perhaps a friend of yours assumes that role. Every group has leaders.

Salvation history has its leaders, too. In the events written about in the Old Testament, God called people like Moses, David, Deborah, and the prophets to be leaders and to maintain the covenant. God often chose unlikely people so that it would be clear to everyone that God's power was behind their actions.

The New Testament tells the story of the new covenant fulfilled through the Son of God. The four Gospels show us how Jesus taught his disciples by using parables and demonstrated the power of his teaching by his actions. Those he called to follow him had to change their lives and live as Jesus did. Jesus sent his apostles and disciples out to tell others the good news of God's kingdom.

The mission of spreading the good news of Jesus continues today in the Church. We are called to be witnesses to Christ, learning from him and sharing his life with others by the way we live.

Reflect on how Jesus' sending forth his apostles and disciples to share the good news applies to your life. Share your thoughts with your Faith Partner.

FaiTH PartNeRSHiP

WRAP UP

- The New Testament is the continuation of the story of salvation history begun in the Old Testament.
- In both the Old and New Testaments, God called people to be great leaders.
- Christians believe that Jesus is the covenant for all people.
- The Gospels tell us that Jesus taught by what he said and did, and that he sent his followers to spread the good news of God's kingdom throughout the world.
- We are called to be disciples of Jesus and to show others how to live according to his teachings.

What questions do you have about this material?

_____

_____

_____

Around the Group

Discuss the following questions as a group.

How does a good leader act? What are some things that a good leader will not ask his or her followers to do?

After everyone has had a chance to share his or her responses, come up with a group answer to the first question upon which everyone can agree.

_____

_____

_____

_____

What personal observations do you have about the group discussion and answer?

_____

_____

_____

_____

_____

Briefly...

At the beginning of this chapter, you were asked what qualities encourage you to think of someone as a leader. Now that you know more about leadership and discipleship, how can you become a better disciple and a better leader?

_____

_____

_____

Applying the Bible Message

Expressions of Faith—

In the New Testament Jesus proclaims the ultimate truth about God: God is love. He was sent by the Father to show us how God wants us to live. Jesus is God's word made human. In the Gospels Jesus teaches us how important it is to live according to his words. Applying the message of the Bible to our lives may be the most basic and important Skill for Christian Living.

Skill Steps—

Remember that applying the Bible message means living according to Jesus' teaching and example.
Here are some key points to remember:

- The Old Testament contains the story of God's relationship with humanity.

- The Jewish people today cherish the Hebrew Scriptures (most of our Old Testament) as the word of God.

- The New Testament contains the story and teachings of Jesus, who saved us from the power of sin and everlasting death and who showed us the way God wants us to live.

- As Christians we study the word of God and apply it to our lives.

- We can apply the Bible message to our conscience, character, contribution, and knowledge of God.

Skill Builder–

The skill of Applying the Bible Message to your life can be found in
Conscience—what is right and what is wrong.
Character—the kind of person you are.
Contribution—what you do to help others.
Knowledge of God—the nature and characteristics of God.

Share your responses and
thoughts with your Faith Partner.

Look up the following passages from the New Testament, and decide to
which of the four areas each passage can be applied. Some passages may
apply to more than one area.

_____ *Matthew 5:27–28*   **a.** Conscience

_____ *Matthew 5:36–37*   **b.** Character

_____ *John 3:16–17*   **c.** Contribution

_____ *John 14:6*   **d.** Knowledge of God

_____ *Galatians 6:10*

_____ *Colossians 3:12–16*

_____ *James 2:14–16*

Putting It into Practice–

You now understand the importance of applying the teaching of the Bible
to your life. Now practice the skill by choosing one of the passages from
the *Skill Builder* exercise. How can you apply the message to your life?
Give specific examples.

_____

_____

As you study the Bible, it is always a good idea to check your interpretation
of Scripture with someone who is more knowledgeable.

In which of the four areas do you most need to improve the way you use
the skill?

_____

Closing Prayer–

O God, in your love for us you give us everything we need to
live our lives fully. We thank you for Jesus, your Word of life,
who guides us and protects us. May we be witnesses to gospel
joy this day and every day of our lives. Amen.

The Teaching Church

Spirit of Holiness, you are present with us throughout all time. Guide your Church to remain faithful to the teachings and example of Jesus. Bless our leaders with wisdom and compassion. Amen.

Think about the question "What has the teaching authority of the Church ever done for me?" Write your response to each of the items below. SA–Strongly Agree, A–Agree, D–Disagree, SD–Strongly Disagree

_____ If it weren't for the Church, I wouldn't be who I am today.

_____ The Church has helped me form my attitudes and values.

_____ Being a member of the Church has helped me grow in love for God.

_____ The values the Church teaches have helped bring out the best in me.

_____ The view the Church takes of the uniqueness and importance of life has helped me appreciate myself and others.

_____ The sacraments of the Church have helped me celebrate my growth as a friend of Jesus.

_____ My involvement with the Church has helped me in my relationships with family and friends.

_____ The Church means little to me.

Authority

Sometimes we feel uncomfortable with authority. Those who have authority over others can be powerfully tempted to abuse or misuse that authority. At times whole nations have suffered at the hands of powerful leaders. The bumper sticker slogan "Question Authority" has its roots in our fear and mistrust of those who have power over us.

True authority is a gift from God. In the creation stories from the Book of Genesis, God gave the first couple dominion over the earth and its creatures. God gave them this power not for them to harm or take advantage of creation, but so that they might nurture and protect it—be good stewards.

The leaders of the Church seek to nurture and protect the members of Christ's Body. Those in authority strive to ensure that all people, powerful and powerless, young and old, have the opportunity to share the good things of creation.

A Certain Something

Have you ever met someone who impressed you right from the start? At first meeting, something about this person seems electric, magnetic. You feel a sense of awe just standing in his or her presence. You will find it hard to look away, and you find yourself believing everything he or she has to say. What makes this person special and believable may be difficult to describe. But one thing you know for sure: this person is for real.

Some of the people who encountered Jesus during his ministry had a similar experience. Naturally, anyone who witnessed Jesus performing a miracle was impressed by his power. But many who listened to his teaching were astonished at what they heard and felt: "They were astounded at his teaching, for he taught them as one having authority, and not as the scribes" *(Mark 1:22)*. In each town Jesus entered, many came to put their faith in him. There was something about Jesus that appealed to people. His words stirred their hearts.

What made Jesus' authority special? He had no title, no uniform, no big money behind him. But he didn't need any of those things. His authority did not come from any person or organization, but from God. Never before had people seen someone with such authority reach out to those who were poor, sinful, sick, and lowly. No wonder people were in awe!

Catholics Believe

All the Christian faithful, both lay and ordained, share in the mission of the Church. See Catechism, #872.

Fill in the blanks of the statement below.

Three ways I can share in the mission of the Church at this time in my life are _____, _____, and
_____.

A Shared Authority

One way to tell a good leader from a bad one is to look at how that person shares authority. A wise leader will share the power of his or her authority among well-trained disciples. A shared authority empowers the group and guarantees that the mission and values of the leader will live on in his or her followers.

Early in his ministry Jesus sent out his disciples two by two on a mission to teach, heal, and cast out demons as he did. (See *Matthew 10:5–15.*) At the Last Supper Jesus promised to send the Holy Spirit to his followers to remain with them after Jesus himself had gone. This Spirit of Truth would enable them to remain faithful to the mission they had received. (See *John 16:5–15.*)

The disciples had everything they needed to continue the saving mission of Jesus after he ascended to heaven. They had the memory of his teachings and his example. They even had his promise of a share in his authority. When the day of Pentecost came, the gifts of the Holy Spirit were released in the disciples. The Church burst forth upon the world in the actions of the apostles. (See *Acts 2.*)

Jesus did not leave his Church without a leader. Throughout his ministry Jesus shared the special moments of his life with his apostles. Among the circle of your friends, you probably have one or two who are closer to you than the rest. You may have known them longer, or maybe they understand you better. When the really significant moments of your life are unfolding, you want to share them with these special friends. For Jesus those special friends were Peter, James, and John. But even among these three, Peter stood out.

Jesus asked the disciples who people thought he was. They gave him multiple answers: John the Baptist, Elijah, or maybe even Jeremiah. Peter alone was single-minded in his reply. "You are the Messiah, the Son of the living God," he declared *(Matthew 16:16).*

Guiding Our Faith The United States National Conference of Catholic Bishops (NCCB) is the organization of bishops who govern the Catholic Church in the United States. This body, formed in 1966 in response to the Second Vatican Council, has its roots in the National Catholic Welfare Council formed in 1919. The NCCB has made major decisions regarding liturgy, sacramental practices, and religious education. The conference has also issued many documents, some of which were intended to guide Catholic youth and Catholic youth ministry. In 1997 the conference issued **Renewing the Vision,** which highlights the many gifts of Catholic youth and the many opportunities available for Catholic youth ministry. Also known by its organizational and public policy wing, the United States Catholic Conference (USCC), the bishops have made important statements regarding nuclear war, the economy, and the sanctity of life.

For further information: To learn more about the service of the NCCB, obtain a copy of **Renewing the Vision,** or look them up on the Internet at **www.nccbuscc.org.**

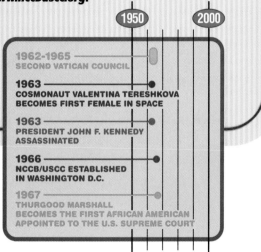

1950 — 2000

1962-1965
SECOND VATICAN COUNCIL

1963
COSMONAUT VALENTINA TERESHKOVA BECOMES FIRST FEMALE IN SPACE

1963
PRESIDENT JOHN F. KENNEDY ASSASSINATED

1966
NCCB/USCC ESTABLISHED IN WASHINGTON D.C.

1967
THURGOOD MARSHALL BECOMES THE FIRST AFRICAN AMERICAN APPOINTED TO THE U.S. SUPREME COURT

Jesus blessed him for this answer. In *Matthew 16:18–19* we read that Jesus said, "You are Peter, and on this rock I will build my church, . . . I will give you the keys of the kingdom of heaven. . . ." (The name *Peter* means "rock.")

Before Jesus returned to his Father, he commissioned his apostles to "Go into all the world and proclaim the good news to the whole creation" *(Mark 16:15)*. Because of this we say that the Church is **apostolic,** founded on the teaching of the apostles. As an apostolic Church we believe that, through the guidance of the Holy Spirit, the Church continues the teaching of the apostles and will continue it until Christ's return.

Sometimes in our relationship with God, we need instructions and guidance. This is the role of the teaching Church. The teaching authority of the Church is called the **magisterium,** which means "body of teachers." The magisterium of the Church today is found in the bishops in union with the pope. Together they guide and teach the rest of the Church. At times the Church's leaders teach with **infallibility.** This means that in some instances they teach a doctrine related to faith or morals and, in doing so, are guided by the Holy Spirit and are protected from error. Though not all Church teaching is considered infallible, all of it is important because it helps us better understand our faith.

Our Church Family

Our Church family is as varied as the world we live in. We most often see our Church represented through its leaders and through our parish community. But the Body of Christ is actually every one of us. We are as much a part of the Church as our adult family members, our priest, and even our pope. All of us have different roles within the Church, but we all work to represent Christ's Body. Together we proclaim the good news, we serve others as a way to help them experience God's love, and we live together in a community of faith, hope, and love. Together we are a community of believers.

As part of the Church community, we also speak of the **domestic Church,** that is, the Church at its most fundamental level within families. The domestic Church is our first teacher in the faith. The family should be the first faith community in which we learn our most valuable lessons. Most of the time our families made the decision to have us baptized as infants. They support our religious instruction in the school or the parish. They teach us by their example what love and faithfulness mean. And they guide us in the formation of our values as disciples of Jesus and in the development of our conscience.

Saint Paul speaks of the Church as the Body of Christ: a body with many members sharing a common life with Christ as our head. Since Paul's time our Church community has grown into a large and complex group. But our goal remains the same—to bring the gospel of Jesus to the world.

opening the Word

Palm Sunday, Cycle C

"... the greatest among you must become like the youngest, and the leader like one who serves." Luke 22:26

Read *Luke 22:24–30* as well as *John 13:3–15* and *1 Corinthians 12:4–13*. Write a brief example of a time when you saw a person in authority lead through an act of service.

_____

_____

_____

_____

Authority to Lead and Teach

At times, the adult who has authority at home, at school, or at work shares his or her authority with you by empowering you to do certain tasks. If you're a responsible leader, you share authority with others. You make sure you responsibly complete the things that have been asked of you.

People could sense God's authority in the power of Jesus' words and actions. Jesus commissioned the apostles, gave them authority, and sent them out to teach in his name.

Today the Church is called apostolic because it is founded on the apostles. The Church teaches with the same power and authority that the apostles received from Jesus. In every generation the Holy Spirit guides the Church so that its teachings are right and true.

The family is the domestic Church. In your family you learn about the faith. You are also guided by what you learn from the magisterium, passed on to you through priests, deacons, and teachers. You, in turn, carry on Jesus' mission when you lead others in the way that Christ taught. In word and action, the whole Church participates in the teaching mission of Jesus.

Reflect on what questions you would like to ask the magisterium. Share your thoughts with your Faith Partner. Create a letter and give it to your teacher.

FaiTH PaRTNeRSHiP

WRAP UP

- Jesus taught with authority that came from God because he was the Son of God.
- Jesus shared his authority with the apostles; they received the courage to teach the gospel from the Holy Spirit.
- The Church is the people of God. It is apostolic because it is founded on the apostles.
- The magisterium of the Church teaches with the authority of Jesus passed down through the apostles.
- Our families are the domestic Church, where we first learn about our faith.
- The whole Church participates in the teaching mission of Jesus.

What questions do you have about the material in this chapter?

_____

_____

_____

Around the Group

Discuss the following questions as a group:

What role does the magisterium play in the lives of people your age? How can members of your parish community help you come to a better understanding of your faith?

After everyone has had a chance to share his or her responses, come up with a group answer for the second question upon which everyone can agree.

_____

_____

_____

What personal observations do you have about the group discussion and answer?

_____

_____

_____

Briefly...

At the beginning of this chapter, you were asked to think about the effect the Church's authority and teachings have had on you. Now that you have learned more about authority, what are the best ways you can use the authority that is given to you?

_____

_____

_____

Discerning What Is Right

Expressions of Faith—

The Church calls us to be courageous disciples and to do what is right. The term *discern* means to decide or recognize. The skill of Discerning What Is Right helps us develop the ability to take a look at a situation and make good decisions. As we learn to discern right and wrong actions, we begin to live safer, more virtuous lives.

Scripture

"But the Advocate, the Holy Spirit, whom the Father will send in my name, will teach you everything, and remind you of all that I have said to you."

John 14:26   6th Sunday of Easter, Cycle C

Think About It—

Read and evaluate each of the following situations.

◯ Julio took his father's car without permission because nobody was home and he wanted to go to the movies.

Did Julio make a good choice? Explain.

_____

_____

◯ Fran's little brother was sick and her mother was working, so Fran stayed home from school and took care of her brother.

Did Fran make a good choice? Explain.

_____

_____

◯ Latisha gave the money to her church when she began to feel bad about taking money from her teacher's desk.

Did Latisha make a good choice? Explain.

_____

_____

Share your responses and thoughts with your Faith Partner.

Skill Steps-

To improve the skill of Discerning What Is Right, you need to consider three things:
The ACT
The INTENTION
The CIRCUMSTANCE

The Church teaches that sometimes an act can be objectively wrong, but the intention of the person committing the wrong act can be a good one, or circumstances may put a wrong act in a different light. For instance, it is wrong to steal. But what if a person who has no money steals a piece of bread in order to feed a starving brother or sister? The intention of the person stealing the bread and the circumstances surrounding the act make a difference. But we must never make intentions and circumstances serve as excuses for doing what we want rather than what is right.

Check It Out-

Place a check mark next to the statements that apply to you.

○ I think most things are either always right or always wrong.

○ I take my time when trying to discern what is right.

○ I quit trying to figure out what the correct answer is if I get too confused.

○ I usually ask what the Church teaches about different moral acts.

○ I usually ask for God's guidance when discerning what is right.

○ I think intentions and circumstances have a lot to do in discerning what's right.

How many did you check? Based on your responses, what kinds of things do you need to work on?

_____

_____

Closing Prayer-

O **God**, because you *love* us, you *guide* us in ways that will lead to our *happiness*. Through your *son* Jesus, you give the Church the *authority* to **teach** what is *right* and **good**. Help us in our *mission* of leading others in the way of *Christ*. Amen.

Professing
Our Faith

God, you reveal yourself to us as the Father of all. In Jesus, you save us from the power of sin and death. By the workings of the Spirit, show us the way to unending joy in your kingdom.

All people are created with equal dignity.
No one should live in want.
Everyone has a right to life, liberty, and the pursuit of happiness.
Human life is sacred.

The statements above are called statements of conviction, or belief, because they are basic rules to live by. What are some of your own statements of conviction?

_____

_____

_____

_____

_____

_____

Convictions

We often use the word *believe* casually—such as when we say "I believe the Yankees are better than the Cubs," or "Can you believe she likes that kind of music?" But other beliefs are so strong that they shape who we are and who we become. These convictions may be so important to us that we live for them and make sacrifices because of them. We may argue with people who disagree with us. We may speak publicly about our convictions to persuade more people to think as we do, such as when people speak out against abortion or discrimination. Sometimes people have even been willing to die for their beliefs, such as the four missionaries who died in El Salvador.

When our convictions lead us to public speech and actions, we become witnesses to what we believe. If we profess our beliefs openly, in words or by example, our witness may affect how others think, feel, and act. This is the basis of living out our faith: conviction that leads to action.

Say It, Live It

People in every age have held powerful convictions that changed their lives and even the course of history. Sometimes people with strong beliefs work for major changes in society, such as the Civil Rights movement of the 1960s. Such public witness may influence others to join and support a cause. On the other hand, publicly expressed convictions that call for a significant change may inspire other people to oppose such a change. For example, pro-democracy demonstrators in China in the late 1980s led to a government crackdown in which thousands of demonstrators are believed to have been imprisoned and killed.

In every generation people have been willing to dedicate their lives to causes such as peace, freedom, justice, equality, and love. Many have shaped their lives and gone to their deaths because of their beliefs in God. What beliefs do you hold that shape the way you live, make decisions, or spend your money and time? How might these beliefs shape your future? What beliefs would you be willing to die for?

Share your thoughts with your Faith Partner.

FaiTH PaRTNeRSHiP

Our Global Community

Doctors Without Borders

Acting on their belief that all people have a right to medical care, doctors formed an organization in 1971 to help victims of war, epidemics, and disasters worldwide. Officially known by the French name, *Medecins San Frontieres (MSF)*, it is the largest independent international medical relief agency, and it depends entirely on volunteers and the support of private donors. At any one time as many as two thousand volunteers serve in more than eighty countries. In 1999 MSF was awarded the Nobel Peace Prize.

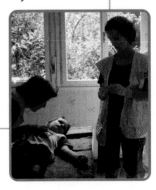

What We Believe

The word *creed* comes from the Latin word *credo,* or "I believe." A man once came to Jesus, begging for his son's healing. Jesus questioned the man's faith. "I believe," the man cried, and added, "Help my unbelief." (See *Mark 9:17–29.*) This honest statement is a profound expression of faith. The father in the story still had many questions, but he knew that his trust in Jesus would save his son.

Many such creeds appear in the New Testament. Peter professed his faith with a simple sentence that earned him praise from Jesus. "You are the Messiah, the Son of the living God" *(Matthew 16:16).* After the resurrection, Thomas doubted the other disciples who said they had seen Jesus. When Jesus appeared before the disciples a second time and Thomas was present, the doubter became a believer with one of the shortest and most famous creeds: "My Lord and my God!" *(John 20:28).*

Saint Paul offered this creed to those who were new in the faith: ". . . if you confess with your lips that Jesus is Lord and believe in your heart that God raised him from the dead, you will be saved" *(Romans 10:9).* Paul wanted the young Church community to know that Christian faith requires both sincere conviction and public witness.

The primary belief of the early Church is still the central mystery of the Catholic faith today: we believe in God the Father, Jesus his Son, and the Holy Spirit. Our belief in the **Holy Trinity** is the basis of every formal creed of the Church.

OUR CHRISTIAN JOURNEY

A New Profession of Faith The year 1968 marked 1,900 years since the martyrdom of Saints Peter and Paul. In honor of the nineteenth centenary anniversary, Pope Paul VI pronounced a new version of the creed at Saint Peter's Basilica. The pope wanted to honor the faith of the original apostles by updating the Nicene Creed with statements addressing how the modern world has affected our spiritual lives. Pope Paul VI's pronouncement, the ***Credo of the People of God,*** has thirteen sections, including such topics as the Trinity, original sin, Baptism, and our hope in the resurrection.

For further information: Find a summary of the document in a Catholic encyclopedia, or research the original text on the Internet.

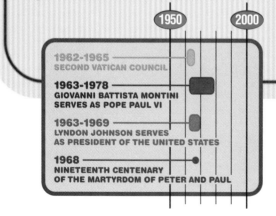

1950   2000

1962-1965
SECOND VATICAN COUNCIL

1963-1978
GIOVANNI BATTISTA MONTINI
SERVES AS POPE PAUL VI

1963-1969
LYNDON JOHNSON SERVES
AS PRESIDENT OF THE UNITED STATES

1968
NINETEENTH CENTENARY
OF THE MARTYRDOM OF PETER AND PAUL

The Apostles' Creed

Sources of information can be unreliable, like gossip or some stories passed around the Internet. Newspapers and news programs usually strive for accuracy, but they are only as good as their sources. It is best to rely on eyewitness sources. The closer you get to a person who was present at the event, the more reliable your information will be.

The Church begins as close to its primary sources as possible when preparing a statement of faith. The **Apostles' Creed** is an important statement because it dates back to the beliefs of the early Church. The Apostles' Creed was probably used in the early centuries of the Church as a profession of faith at the time of Baptism.

The Apostles' Creed has three main parts, corresponding to the three Persons of the Trinity. In the opening section we as believers make several *affirmations,* or pronouncements, about God. After first stating that we believe in God, we acknowledge God as Father, Almighty, and Creator of all things.

The second part of the Creed contains statements of our belief in Jesus. Jesus is called Christ, the Son of God, and Lord. His divinity is also expressed by our acknowledgment of his conception through the power of the Holy Spirit. His humanity is affirmed in the statement that he is the son of the Virgin Mary. The Creed recognizes the mystery of his suffering, death, resurrection, and ascension. Finally, Jesus is acknowledged as the judge of the living and the dead.

The third part of the Apostles' Creed affirms our Christian belief in the Holy Spirit. It also highlights our faith in the Church, the communion of the faithful both living and dead, God's forgiveness, and our hope in the resurrection and everlasting life.

Catholics Believe

There is but one God, three Persons but one essence. See Catechism, #202.

Write your own creed on what you believe about the Trinity.

_____

_____

_____

_____

The Nicene Creed

The **Nicene Creed** we recite at Mass is an expanded version of the Apostles' Creed. It is more properly known as the "Nicene-Constantinopolitan Creed" because it was developed in Constantinople in A.D. 381 using an earlier Creed from the Church Council of Nicaea in A.D. 325. The Nicene Creed has been the official Creed of the Church since the sixth century.

The Nicene Creed follows the Trinitarian formula of the Apostles' Creed, but it is longer and includes more detail. The council that created this new Creed used it to clarify some key ideas about the Trinity that were causing disagreement and confusion among Christians. For example, in the first section of the Creed, God is referred to as "one God." The council at Constantinople wished to make clear that belief in the Trinity is not belief in three gods.

Another example is in the section about Jesus. Was he human or was he divine? The answer: he was both. As the Creed states, Jesus was "true God from true God" but he was also "born of the Virgin Mary, and became man."

The Nicene Creed expands the idea of the Holy Spirit, as well. The Spirit is called "the giver of life," in union with the creative activity of the Father and the Son. The Holy Spirit is identified as the voice of God who spoke through the prophets.

One Faith

Both Creeds are intended to help Christians understand their beliefs. Using two Creeds might seem confusing at first. But each Creed is meant to focus our attention on the same aspects of our faith, while emphasizing different things.

In union with our families and our Church community, we use the Apostles' Creed and the Nicene Creed to profess our beliefs—to proclaim our convictions loud and clear.

Opening the Word

Passion (Palm) Sunday

. . . every tongue should confess that Jesus Christ is Lord, to the glory of God the Father.
Philippians 2:11

Read *Philippians 2:6–11*, a passage sometimes called the Hymn to Christ, as well as *Romans 10:8–13* and *1 Corinthians 15:3–4*. What beliefs about Jesus are being affirmed in these passages?

_____

_____

_____

The Power of Belief

The precise expression of what we believe comes from the early centuries of the Church. The Apostles' Creed and the Nicene Creed both express the belief that there is one God in three divine Persons: Father, Son, and Holy Spirit. Affirmations about the Trinity are included, along with our beliefs about Baptism, forgiveness, resurrection, and the Church.

The way we live reveals our beliefs to others. We may say that we believe in taking care of the environment or that those people who lack many of the privileges most people take for granted deserve equal treatment. But only when we decide to speak and act for change are we really expressing our beliefs. We can wear T-shirts with socially conscious messages on them or say that we support a cause because we use its screensaver. But it is more important to actually do something to change the situation.

Religious beliefs work the same way. What we believe about God and human life needs to be expressed in our words and actions. Our beliefs can be powerful enough to cause dramatic change in our lives and to affect the lives of people around us. Throughout history certain beliefs and the actions they inspired altered the course of world events. Through our words and actions we can become witnesses to our faith in God.

Reflect on the importance of expressions of faith in our lives. Share your thoughts with your Faith Partner.

FaiTH ParTNeRSHiP

WRAP UP

- **Faith is belief that leads to expression of our faith in words and actions.**
- **Beliefs shape our lives and determine how we live and who we become.**
- **We believe in one God as a Trinity of Persons: Father, Son, and Holy Spirit.**
- **The Apostles' Creed and the Nicene Creed express our Christian beliefs.**
- **Both Creeds express our faith in the Trinity, the Church, Baptism, forgiveness, and resurrection.**

What questions do you have about the material in this chapter?

_____

_____

_____

Around the Group

Discuss the following as a group.

Choose one statement from the Apostles' Creed and one from the Nicene Creed. How, through words and actions, do we express each statement?

After everyone has had a chance to share his or her responses, come up with a group answer regarding one of the statements upon which everyone can agree.

_____
_____
_____
_____

What personal observations do you have about the group discussion?

_____
_____
_____
_____

Briefly...

At the beginning of this chapter, you were asked to list your statements of conviction. Based on what you have written, create a statement that includes what you think the Church might add.

_____
_____
_____

SKILLS FOR Christian Living

Discerning What Is Right

Expressions of Faith—

We express our faith not only by what we say, but also by how we live. In the Gospels, Jesus taught that people would know us by the fruits of our lives. (See *Matthew 7:16–20*.) Your life is your faith in action. The Nicene Creed says that the Holy Spirit is the giver of life. The Holy Spirit will help you choose and discern what is right.

Skill Steps—

Remember that the skill of Discerning What Is Right helps us live as Jesus taught us. Consider three things when discerning what is right: the ACT, the INTENTION, and the CIRCUMSTANCE.

Here are some key points to remember:

● The magisterium teaches us doctrine and objective moral reasoning (certain acts are wrong no matter what).

● We express our faith by our beliefs and our decisions.

● Discerning what's right and having the courage to stand by your decisions takes practice and prayer.

● Even good acts lose their goodness if practiced with poor intentions or self-serving circumstances.

ACT
INTENTION
CIRCUMSTANCE

Skill Builder-

Choose your most likely response:

Share your responses and thoughts with your Faith Partner.

1. A friend tells a racist joke. Your friends think it is funny, but you refuse to laugh. Do you:
   - ◯ Walk away
   - ◯ Confront your friend, expressing your objection to the racist joke

   Why did you choose what you did? Was it the act, the intention, or the circumstance that helped you make your decision? Explain.

   _____

2. The older brother of a friend offers to show you and your friend pornographic sites on the Internet. Do you:
   - ◯ Tell him you don't have time right now and leave
   - ◯ Tell your parents

   Why did you choose what you did? Was it the act, the intention, or the circumstance that helped you make your decision? Explain.

   _____

Putting It into Practice-

Now use your skill at discerning by recalling a time when you had to make a difficult decision.

What was the situation? _____

What did you intend by the act? _____

What was the circumstance that motivated you to do what you did?

_____

Was it the act, the intention, or the circumstance that influenced

you the most? _____

Would you change anything if you could? If so, what? _____

_____

Throughout our lives we will constantly be forced to make decisions. The key in making good decisions is discerning what is right and following through with our actions.

Closing Prayer-

*O God, you are the Creator of us all. By the **power** of the Holy Spirit, you give us life and guide us in the way of faith. Help us always to live by what we believe. Amen*

Celebrating *in* **Community**

Giver of Life, you saw that it was not good for us to be alone. Through Jesus, you welcome us into the community of faith. By the Spirit's power, sustain your Church in holiness and unity. Amen.

Circle the communities to which you belong.

family

neighborhood

team

parish

scout troop

band

choir

Reflect for a moment on the events you celebrate with each of these groups and what form these celebrations take. Choose the group with which you feel the most unity and explain why.

_____

_____

_____

_____

Unity

Before a lone clarinet player joins the band, the music of the small reed instrument may sound thin and incomplete. But together with other clarinets, not to mention oboes and drums and brass and cymbals, the sound of the music swells and creates wonderful harmonies. As they join together, the many voices of the instruments become one.

When we work together as a community, we speak with one voice about our common values and concerns. Individually, we may feel powerless to face natural disasters, world hunger, or even local injustices. But when many people work as one unit, seemingly impossible tasks become possible.

Jesus understood this when he gathered his followers. An important feature of his group was its unity, bringing together people from different backgrounds. Though they were many, they came to recognize their oneness. Out of this community, our Church came to be.

Time to Celebrate

Usually when it's time to celebrate, people come together. Holidays, family reunions, and gatherings of friends all share certain features. The mood is happy. People are glad to see each other. We often share food, and we may play special music to mark the season or occasion. Overall, we are thankful for our relationships, for the time to enjoy one another's company, and for the love that brings this community together.

The signs of celebration—joy, food, and gratitude—are present when the Church gathers, too. The word *church* means "assembly" or "gathering." The Church by definition reflects the understanding that we are social beings by nature. Even Jesus traveled with a group of disciples, and when the time came for him to return to the Father, he sent the Holy Spirit to support and strengthen the group. (See *John 20:19–23*.)

The early Christian community was marked by the spirit of joy. It became their custom to share what they had with others, and together they celebrated their faith at the Eucharistic meal. Rich and poor, Jew and Gentile, male and female, slave and free citizen, all came together to celebrate the faith that made them one.

Catholics Believe

The word church designates the worshiping assembly, but also the local community, and believers everywhere. See Catechism, #752.

What is the name of the local community you think of as your "church"? For example, you might respond, "I am a member of Saint Albert the Great parish." How does your local Church community show that it is part of the larger Church of believers?

_____

_____

_____

We Celebrate as One

The common meal was a significant event for this community. At the Last Supper, Jesus told his disciples to remember him in the breaking of the sacred Bread and the sharing of the sacred Wine. (See *Luke 22:14–20.*) After the resurrection, some travelers along the road to Emmaus met Jesus, though they did not recognize him at first. It was only when they stopped to rest and shared bread and wine with this stranger that they realized he was Jesus. (See *Luke 24:13–35.*) From the earliest record we have in the Acts of the Apostles, sacred Bread and sacred Wine were shared among Christians. Like the travelers to Emmaus, our eyes are opened to Christ's presence among us when we share this sacred meal together.

Our word *Eucharist* comes from a Greek word that means "to give thanks." When Christians gather, it is always time to give thanks. We are grateful for the love of God shown to us in Jesus. We give thanks for God's Spirit who lives in our hearts and guides the Church. Our gratitude for Christ's victory over the power of sin and the promise of eternal life gives us every reason to celebrate.

All celebrations have *rituals,* or meaningful actions that are repeated at each gathering. Baseball games ritually begin with the singing of the national anthem. When we gather with our friends, we may sometimes eat the same foods and listen to our favorite music. In the last section of the Nicene Creed, we profess that we believe in "one, holy, catholic, and apostolic church." Because we are *one,* our unity is an essential part of our celebration as Church. The signs we use in our rituals reflect that oneness. We hold to one faith, which comes to us through the stories of the Old and New Testaments. We believe in one Lord, whom we celebrate in every gathering. We admit new members to the Church under one baptism. "One faith, one Lord, one baptism" is a simple definition of the Christian life, according to Saint Paul. (See *Ephesians 4:1–6.*)

Media Message

THE WORLD COMMUNITY Through the Internet, we can come in contact with people, services, and information from all over the world. Using the Internet, research the Church in another country. Compare similarities and differences with the Church as you experience it.

The Books of Our Celebration The Roman Missal was first promoted in 1570 by Pope Pius V after the Council of Trent. The original Roman Missal, written in Latin, contained the prayers and Scripture readings for the Mass. After the Second Vatican Council, the Roman Missal was revised and separated into two books. The book with the prayers used during the Mass is called the Sacramentary. The book that contains the Scripture readings for the Mass is called the Lectionary. Both books, issued in the language of the people, are used during our celebration of the Eucharist.

For further information: Ask to see the Sacramentary and Lectionary at your parish. Spend some time familiarizing yourself with their contents.

The Church uses particular signs to celebrate the presence of Jesus among us. These ritual actions, called sacraments, are signs of God's love and sources of grace. All seven sacraments—Baptism, Confirmation, Eucharist, Reconciliation, the Anointing of the Sick, Matrimony, and Holy Orders—are occasions to celebrate our unity with Christ and one another.

The three Sacraments of Christian Initiation, Baptism, Confirmation, and Eucharist, draw us into full participation in the life of Christ. They also make us full members of the Church.

The two Sacraments of Healing, Reconciliation and the Anointing of the Sick, remind us that sin and everlasting death have been overcome by the power of God's forgiveness. No longer can spiritual or physical forces separate us from God's love if we, like the Prodigal Son, choose to turn homeward. (See *Luke 15:11–32*.)

The two Sacraments of Service, Matrimony and Holy Orders, are also witnesses to the Church's spirit of unity. The love between a man and a woman joined in marriage is like the love that Christ bears for his Church, Saint Paul tells us. (See *Ephesians 5:31–32*.) In Holy Orders, the *laying on of hands* symbolizes outpouring of the Spirit and the Spirit's gifts for ministry. From the first generation of Christians until now, the leadership of the Church has been united under the indivisible authority of Christ.

Reflect on your first celebration of the Eucharist. Share your thoughts with your Faith Partner.

We Celebrate the Mystery

The center of Christian belief is the **Paschal mystery,** which refers to Jesus' suffering, death, and resurrection. The word *paschal* comes from the Hebrew word for "passover"—in this case, Jesus' passover from death to life. The Paschal mystery is at the heart of every sacramental celebration of the Church. We participate in this Paschal mystery as we die to sin and rise to new life with Jesus who saved us. We also live this Paschal mystery in the suffering and pain of ordinary living. We know that, with Jesus, we too will experience new life.

In the Mass, we celebrate the Paschal mystery in two ways, in word and sacrament. The **Liturgy of the Word,** which is the first great part of the Mass, includes the readings from Scripture, the homily, and the *General Intercessions,* the prayers for the whole Church. In the second great part of the Mass, the **Liturgy of the Eucharist,** the Paschal mystery is present to us in the form of bread and wine, which we profess in faith as the Body and Blood of Christ. The Liturgy of the Eucharist includes the Preparation of the Gifts, the Eucharistic Prayer, and Communion.

The term *Eucharist* can also be used to refer to the entire Mass. When we celebrate the Eucharist, we celebrate our oneness as Christ's Body, the Church.

Our Holy Communion

The Church is one. As people made in the image and likeness of God, our unity as Church reflects the communion the three Persons of the Holy Trinity share. Though we are many, we are called into "holy communion" with one another. Nothing can separate us, joined by Baptism into one faith under one Lord. Nor can we be separated from the love of God which comes to us in Christ.

Opening the Word

7th Sunday of Easter, Cycle A

"Holy Father, protect them in your name that you have given me, so that they may be one, as we are one." John 17:11

Read *John 17* as well as *Ephesians 2:19–22* and *Philippians 2:1–5.* Make a list of some things that are necessary for Christian unity.

_____

_____

_____

_____

Joyfully We **Belong**

Your circle of friends is special to you. It's made up of different kinds of people, but all of you have something in common, some quality that draws you together and makes you one. You like each other, you do things together, and you share a story. You look forward to being together because these relationships give you a sense of belonging. Your friends can be like a second family. When you get together, and especially when you have good news to share, you celebrate.

Our Church is the gathering of many different kinds of people who joyfully celebrate our unity in Jesus Christ. We use signs, symbols, and rituals to express our oneness. We share one faith, one Lord, and one Baptism. The sacraments of the Church are ritual celebrations of our unity with God in Jesus Christ. Through these seven signs we commemorate the Paschal mystery of Christ's suffering, death, and resurrection. In the Liturgies of the Word and Eucharist at Mass, we celebrate our oneness as Christ's Body.

In all these rituals we express our holy communion with God and with each other. Just as there is one God in three divine Persons, so there is one Church of many members.

Reflect on the things we share with other members of the Body of Christ. Share your thoughts with your Faith Partner.

FaiTH PaRTNeRSHiP

WRAP UP

- Through our faith in Jesus Christ, we gather into one Church and are made one in Baptism.

- We use signs and rituals to celebrate our unity with God and with each other.

- The seven sacraments are ways in which we experience the saving power of the Paschal mystery.

- In the Liturgy of the Word and the Liturgy of the Eucharist, we celebrate our oneness as the Body of Christ.

- The Church reflects the communion shared by the three Persons of the Holy Trinity.

What questions do you have about the information presented in this chapter?

_____

_____

_____

Around the Group

Discuss the following question as a group.

Make a list of the talents and gifts of the people in your group. How does this diversity of gifts make your group and class more whole?

After everyone has had a chance to share his or her responses, come up with a group answer upon which everyone can agree.

_____

_____

_____

_____

What personal observations do you have about the group discussion and answer?

_____

_____

_____

_____

Briefly...

At the beginning of this chapter, you were asked to circle the names of the communities to which you belong. Now that you have learned more about community, which one of the communities you circled at the beginning of the chapter contributes the most to who you are as a person?

_____

_____

_____

Reverencing the Ordinary

Expressions of Faith—

Because ordinary people make up the Church, we recognize holiness in ordinary happenings. In the sacraments we use ordinary water, oil, bread, and wine to celebrate God's presence in our lives, yet they take on special significance for us. Through the fruits of the Holy Spirit, we can see signs of God's presence in our lives through things we would normally consider ordinary.

Scripture

. . . the fruit of the Spirit is love, joy, peace, patience, kindness, generosity, faithfulness, gentleness, and self-control.

Galatians 5:22–23   Pentecost, Cycle B

Think About It—

If you were blindfolded, what fruits could you recognize just by tasting them? List them here.

_____

_____

Give an example of the difference between recognizing a fruit of the Holy Spirit and tasting it. (Tasting it means taking it inside, letting it affect you in some way instead of just looking at it as it sits outside you. Think of the difference between taking a bite of an apple instead of just looking at it on the table.)

_____

_____

_____

_____

_____

_____

_____

The Present is sacred
the ordinary is Holy

Skill Steps

Like any other fruit, the fruits of the Holy Spirit are meant to be enjoyed. These fruits are real human qualities that enrich our lives. We only truly practice the skill of Reverencing the Ordinary when we taste the fruits of the Spirit—when we take them in and savor them, and let God know how much we like them.

Memorize the fruits of the Spirit now, as listed in Paul's Letter to the Galatians on the previous page.

You can taste the fruits of the Holy Spirit every day by reverencing the things and events of ordinary life. And you can continually let God know how much you appreciate these good human qualities when you see them. For those who love God, the present is sacred, and the ordinary is holy. Wherever we are, whatever we're doing, God's Spirit is with us.

After each story below write the fruit of the Spirit that the character is practicing.

1. Jon's mother works at the customer service desk of a local store. All day long people complain to her. Some are rude, yet she never treats anyone rudely in return. _____

2. Even during final exams, when everyone else is nervous and anxious, Ernesto stays calm. He seems to have an inner confidence that things will turn out okay no matter what. _____

Check It Out

Place a check mark next to each of the following statements that apply to you:

◯ I thank God every day for ordinary things.

◯ I usually treat the present as sacred and the ordinary as holy.

◯ I usually recognize the fruit of the Holy Spirit in the ordinary.

◯ I am good at taking in fruits of the Holy Spirit and letting them affect me, instead of just recognizing them.

Based on your response, how well do you revere the ordinary?

_____

Closing Prayer

O God, each day you come to us in the joyful gathering of Church, the celebration of the sacraments, and the ordinary things of our lives. Give us the awareness to always sense that you are with us. Amen.

Living
Faithfully

God, you
created the
world and
called it good.
You made us to
be your holy
people and to
share in the
goodness of
creation.
Help us live
as faithful
members of
our Church
community.

54

Read through the reflection below and circle the phrases that answer the question for you.

When someone is described to you as holy, what is your first impression of that person?

not much fun   pious   does what's right

lover of God   cares for others

hard to relate to   lives life to its fullest

wears a halo   does good works

prays a lot   a nun or priest

How would you feel if someone called you holy, and why?

_____

_____

Being **Holy**

Holiness is said to be a quality of people who lead exceptionally virtuous lives. The Church honors some holy people by naming them saints and celebrating feast days in their honor. Sculptors and artists have traditionally created works of art depicting saints, often indicating the saint's holiness by placing a halo around his or her head. All this attention may lead us to believe that the special relationship saints have with God is not possible for the rest of us.

But when we look closely, the saints' lives are not so different from our own. Saint Francis of Assisi was a fun-loving and carefree young man. Saint Teresa of Ávila often spoke jokingly about her conversations with God.

Saints, like the rest of us, learn from their failures. Their biographies tell the stories of people excited about life and brimming with intense feelings and often brave deeds. Through the lives of the saints, we learn that holiness is an adventurous journey.

God's Holy People

Many images of holiness can be seen in stained-glass windows and on holy cards, so it is hard to imagine holiness in action. We see images of people on their knees praying, like Jesus in the Garden of Gethsemane. We look at statues, such as Michelangelo's *Pieta*, and see the sadness and pain on the faces of Mary, Mary Magdalene, and the male figure (possibly Nicodemus) as they hold the body of Jesus. We have pictures of saints in prayer, their eyes fixed on a sight far beyond this world. We even have pictures that depict saints as they sacrificed their lives for their faith.

Holy images like these have a special story to tell and were originally very helpful as illustrations for religious instruction when most people couldn't read, and there were few books for those who could. A statue, stained-glass window, or portrait of a holy person was a religious textbook for many people in the Middle Ages. People learned to identify the person represented by what he or she was doing or perhaps by what he or she was holding. But a single image could never teach the full story of a holy person or give the full explanation of holiness.

Catholics Believe

Within the communion of saints, both living and dead, we share in "holy gifts" for God's holy people. See Catechism, #948.

Write a prayer to any member of the communion of saints, and ask him or her to help you with a problem or a concern you are experiencing.

_____

_____

_____

A Holy Church

To get another idea about what holiness is, we can look at the lives of virtuous people around us. The Church teaches that the **communion of saints** includes all members of the Church, those who are living on earth and those who are in purgatory or heaven. It may be difficult at first to imagine belonging to a club that includes the apostles, Joan of Arc, Thomas Aquinas, and Kateri Tekakwitha. But this community may also include your great-grandfather, whom you never met, and your aunt, who visits your house regularly. The communion of saints may include your friends, the elderly couple who lives down the street, and people of other countries and centuries who are strangers to you. The communion of saints is larger than time and space.

MATTHEW

JOHN

LUKE

MARK

All who are baptized are God's holy people and belong to a Church that is holy. The word *holy* means "hallowed," or set apart for God. We speak of holy days as those set apart to make us especially mindful of God. Holy water is set apart to be used for blessings. Holy oil is used to *consecrate* those who are anointed with it, setting the anointed ones apart for a particular mission or signifying healing. Holy places, like churches and shrines, are blessed to honor God, who will be worshiped in the rituals of faith that will take place there.

The Church *canonizes* people as saints to recognize and honor their lives and actions as holy. The lives of the saints are models for us to follow. For example, John Bosco is a famous saint who dedicated his life to helping underprivileged youth in his native Italy. Rather than talking down to them, he approached the children on their level. He often used magic tricks and juggling to capture their attention, after which he would talk to them about the gospel. Are there opportunities for you to help other youth in your community?

The **sanctoral cycle** is the calendar of saints' feast days that the Church celebrates throughout the year. The more familiar feast days are Saint Patrick's Day on March 17 and Saint Nicholas's Day on December 6. But lesser-known saints are also honored in the sanctoral cycle. Andrew Dung-Lac and 110 other Vietnamese who were put to death for their faith between 1745 and 1862 share a feast day on November 24. Katharine Drexel, a United States heiress of the nineteenth century, dedicated her life to defending and educating African Americans and Native Americans. She was declared a saint in 2000, and her feast is celebrated on March 3.

Rite Response

Litany of the Saints

A *litany* is a form of prayer that consists of a series of statements to each of which those gathered respond. The Litany of the Saints, which is prayed on Holy Saturday during the Easter Vigil, consists of the naming of a series of holy people, followed by a series of petitions. Those gathered respond to each name and petition appropriately. The Litany of the Saints is another way we are reminded how the communion of saints can help us.

Some canonized saints are remembered because they lived holy lives, and others because they died for their faith. A person who is killed for being a follower of Jesus is called a **martyr.** Father Maximilian Kolbe and Edith Stein are two examples of martyrs from the twentieth century who have been named saints. Many other people died for their faith during the previous century, such as Archbishop Oscar Romero and missionaries in Central America, Africa, India, and Indonesia—some of whom are being considered for canonization.

Mary is first among the communion of saints and the Mother of the Church, because through her the Son of God came into the world to save us. She is our Mother in faith, who shows us by her willing example how to put our trust in God. Three holy days of obligation celebrated in the United States are devoted to Mary: Solemnity of Mary the Mother of God (January 1), Assumption (August 15), and Immaculate Conception (December 8). Among other feasts that honor Mary are Our Lady of the Rosary (October 7) and Our Lady of Guadalupe (December 12).

ADVENT
ADVENT
ORDINARY TIME
INCARNATION
PENTECOST
EASTER
RESURRECTION
ORDINARY TIME

COME, HOLY SPIRIT

OUR CHRISTIAN JOURNEY

A Life of Virtue In the later part of the fourteenth century, a movement for spiritual renewal began in the Netherlands and spread throughout Germany. It was started by Geert de Groote and was known as the Spirituality of the Modern Devotion. The most famous book to emerge from that movement was written by a student of de Groote's named Thomas à Kempis. Unlike many other famous books from the Church history, **The Imitation of Christ** was directed at everyday people who were trying to live virtuous lives. The first two sections of the book offer basic advice on how to live as Christ taught. The third section contains conversations between a holy person and Jesus. And the fourth section offers devotional meditations.

For further information: Visit a Catholic bookstore and review the kinds of books listed under the heading "spirituality."

1350
1450

1350
EDWARD III BEGINS RESTORING WINDSOR CASTLE

c.1380-1471
THOMAS À KEMPIS'S LIFE

1431
JOAN OF ARC MARTYRED

c.1455
GUTENBERG BIBLE COMPLETED

CHRISTMAS

ORDINARY TIME

LENT

TRIDUUM

CYCLE

Our Year of **Faith**

The lives of the canonized saints have much to teach us about growing in holiness. But we, like the saints themselves, turn first to the life of Jesus for an example of how to live faithfully. The Church uses a calendar called the **liturgical year** for recognizing and following the annual cycle that celebrates Christ's life, death, resurrection, and ascension. The liturgical year does not run from January to December as the traditional secular calendar does. It begins in late November or early December with the Season of Advent. During Advent the Church prepares to celebrate the birth of Jesus, the *incarnation,* and anticipates Christ's second coming at the end of time. The liturgical year ends in late November on the Feast of Christ the King.

Opening the Word

9th Sunday of Ordinary Time, Cycle A

"Not everyone who says to me, 'Lord, Lord,' will enter the kingdom of heaven, but only the one who does the will of my Father in heaven." Matthew 7:21

Read *Matthew 7* as well as *Matthew 6:5–6* and *Luke 6:20–31.* Design a billboard slogan based on one of the Scripture statements.

Share your design with your Faith Partner.

FaiTH PaRTNeRSHiP

The liturgical year also includes the other major Seasons of Christmas, Lent, and Easter, as well as the Triduum, Solemnity of Pentecost, and Ordinary Time. During Ordinary Time we reflect on what it means to be a disciple of Jesus.

Called to Be **Saints**

From season to season and year to year, we are called to live lives of holiness. We may not be called personally to be martyrs for our faith, and most of us will not make the canon of saints celebrated in the sanctoral cycle. But holiness is our common vocation as members of the Church. The communion of saints is the first and final community to which we belong.

The Call to Holiness

As members of the Church, we share in its holiness. To be holy is to be set apart for God's purposes. Somewhat like the holy water we use for blessing or the holy oil we use for anointing, we are holy people whom God uses for his work. This is the real meaning of sainthood.

Whether or not we recognize it, every decision we make affects the whole community. Because each of us is a member of the communion of saints, we can draw strength from one another and from those who have gone before us. If we make a virtuous decision, such as choosing to spend time with a friend who is depressed, we strengthen our community. In the same way, if we choose to ignore the friend who is in trouble, we hurt him or her and we weaken our community.

To adapt a line from a well-known saying, the journey to sainthood begins with the first step—and it continues one step at a time. When you compare your past actions or your recent choices to the lives of saints, you may think that you could never be as holy or as virtuous as they were. But remember, most of the saints you look up to simply made a series of choices similar to the ones you are faced with every day. They chose to follow Jesus' teachings and live the gospel message through their actions. What will you do?

Reflect with your Faith Partner on how everything that we do, whether charitable or sinful, affects the whole community.

FaiTH ParTNeRSHiP

WRAP UP

- The Church is holy, and all the members of the Church are called to be holy.
- To be holy is to be set apart for God's purposes.
- The holiness of the saints is shown by the fruitfulness of their lives.
- The communion of saints includes all the members of the Church, both living on earth and those in purgatory and heaven.
- The holiness of canonized saints is celebrated in the sanctoral calendar.

What questions do you have about what you studied in this chapter?

_____

_____

_____

Dear Madeline,
Thank you for stopping by this weekend!
love,
Grandma

Around the Group

Discuss the following question as a group.

What responsibilities do you have as a member of the communion of saints?

After everyone has had a chance to share his or her responses, come up with a group answer upon which everyone can agree.

_____

_____

What personal observations do you have about the group discussion and answer?

_____

_____

Briefly...

At the beginning of this chapter, you were asked to consider what the word *holy* means. Based on what you have learned in the chapter, describe a holy person whom you admire.

_____

_____

_____

_____

Reverencing the Ordinary

Expressions of Faith—

As members of the Church, we are called to holiness. Together with all the saints, we gather at Mass on Sundays and holy days to give thanks for God's grace working in our lives. Saints point out to us the power of God in the ordinary events of everyday life, just as Jesus did.

Skill Steps—

Remember that reverencing the ordinary involves "tasting" the fruits of the Holy Spirit and letting God know how good these fruits are. We reverence the ordinary by discovering and experiencing qualities or fruits of the Spirit—love, joy, peace, patience, kindness, generosity, faithfulness, gentleness, and self-control—in everyday events.

Here are some key points to remember:

- We have been taught how to reverence that which is holy.

- The saints lived their lives reverencing the ordinary.

- Reverencing the ordinary gives you a rich spiritual life in which happiness does not come from money, power, or popularity.

- As Catholics we practice reverencing the ordinary together through our communal celebrations, such as the sacraments, the liturgy, our songs, and our prayers.

love

joy

kindness

generosity

The Present is Sacred the Ordinary is Holy

Skill Builder-

Develop the skill of Reverencing the Ordinary by identifying which fruit of the Spirit is present in each of the following situations. Write the name of the fruit or quality on the line below each statement.

- While in the gym, Caitlin saw that a fight was about to start, so she went over and calmed everybody down.

  _____

- When José saw that James had forgotten his lunch and didn't have any money, he gave James half his sandwich.

  _____

Share your responses and thoughts with your Faith Partner.

Putting It into Practice-

Now use your ability to reverence the ordinary.

- Describe an event in your life when you had a strong taste of a fruit of the Holy Spirit.

  _____

  _____

- Write a short prayer of thanksgiving to God for that quality.

  _____

  _____

- Write about something you expect to happen tomorrow for which you will need the fruits of the Holy Spirit.

  _____

  _____

- Write a brief prayer asking God to produce in you the qualities that you will need tomorrow.

  _____

  _____

Closing Prayer-

Oh God, how wonderful and good are all the things you do for us. You always take care of us, Lord, and give us what we need to be holy as you are holy. Lead us through our day. In union with Mary and all the saints, may we be faithful members of your holy Church. Amen.

CHAPTER

7

The Church Alive

Lord, you gave us our families to be our first teachers. You gave us the Church to help us grow in faith. We praise you.

Answer the following questions "Yes," "No," or "Not Sure."

_____ Being Catholic keeps me from enjoying life.

_____ I know that I want to be a Catholic for the rest of my life.

_____ I would not mind being a Catholic if the Church would change some of its rules.

_____ It doesn't matter what kind of church you belong to, as long as you believe in God.

_____ I can worship God by myself. I don't need a community.

_____ A lot of people who never practice their faith claim to be Catholic.

_____ In ten years I will be the same kind of Catholic that I am now.

We Are the Church

Your Baptism made you a member of a Church community that extends around the world—to Puerto Rico, Moscow, Australia, Nigeria, and everywhere in between. But the Church is also present for you on a more personal level within your parish community and your family. On a global and local level, the Church is a relationship.

You've probably heard the term *universal*. But what does that mean? On the one hand, universal means big—certainly bigger than just our world. But if something is universal, it is also present everywhere in everything. Through the universality of the Church, each member of the Church experiences the glory of Christ in every part of his or her life. And through our relationships with Christ and with one another, the Church, both globally and locally, becomes present to us. It comes alive.

What's in a Name?

How did you get your name? Were you named for a family member, a famous person, a hero?

In the early days of the Church, followers of Jesus' teachings were called "People of the Way," because Jesus told them, "I am the way, and the truth, and the life" *(John 14:6)*. The name *Christian* was soon given to those who followed Christ. Today all who put their faith in Jesus are happy to bear that name.

In his letters, Ignatius of Antioch (c. 35–c. 107) referred to the Church as catholic. **Catholic** means "universal." The Church in Ignatius's time was spreading far and wide, yet the same faith, the same Lord, and the same Baptism were being proclaimed wherever Christians went.

The term *Roman Catholic,* though never an official name for the Church, came into use at the time of the East-West Schism, which began in the eleventh century. The leaders of the Church in the East chose to be called Orthodox, and the Church in the West, led by the bishop of Rome, continued to use the name Catholic.

Share with your Faith Partner ways in which you express your faith as a Christian.

Our Global Community

Pax Christi

Pax Christi International is a Catholic organization devoted to creating a peaceful world community based on the message of the gospel. Its members sponsor justice and reconciliation efforts which support demilitarization, economic equality, and human rights activities. Pax Christi International includes member organizations from Europe, Asia, Africa, Australia, and North America—including Pax Christi USA.

Each bishop governs a specific area, called a diocese. Each diocese is further divided into parishes. Most parishes are led by a priest who is the pastor, and, at times by other priests and deacons as well. Non-ordained leaders, too, have important responsibilities in many parishes. Many of the people in charge of schools, music and liturgy, and youth ministry in parishes are lay people or members of religious communities. Each member of the Church can have a role in leading and serving its members.

Parishes are the heart of the Christian community. In our parishes we worship, celebrate the sacraments, learn the stories of salvation, and socialize with the community. Many parishes are communities that challenge their members to grow in their faith and to respond to God's call to work for justice.

The most important teachers in the Church may be within the Catholic home, the domestic Church. Ideally it is from our family members that we learn our most valuable lessons about what it means to love, share, serve, and believe. Families should support each other in good times and in bad. Above all, families should be the primary example of a community of faith.

Who We Are Today

In the time of the early Church, Rome was the center of the world. Both Peter and Paul traveled there to help spread the gospel, and both were martyred there. As the heart of human culture, commerce, and politics, Rome was the natural place to plant the seed of Christianity.

Today Rome is the center of Catholicism. Vatican City, the world's smallest sovereign state, is the home of the pope, and many Church offices are located there. Though the pope, who is the bishop of Rome, is in Vatican City, the *college of bishops* is worldwide.

Catholics Believe

The Church is catholic and missionary by its nature.
See Catechism, #868.

How are you a missionary for Christ and the Church?

_____

_____

_____

A Patient Saint Saint Monica is best known as the mother of another more famous saint, Augustine of Hippo. But Monica could also be known as the domestic Church in action. She lived in North Africa in the fourth century and raised her family while never forgetting the needs of those who were poor. When young Augustine chose a sinful and scandalous lifestyle, she prayed constantly for his conversion. Because of her prayers and good example, her husband, mother-in-law, and son all became Christians. Saint Monica is the patron saint of married women. Her feast day is August 27.

For more information: Find three more facts about the life of Saint Monica.

| 300 | | 425 |

313
EDICT OF MILAN

c.330
CONSTRUCTION OF THE FIRST
SAINT PETER'S BASILICA COMPLETED

c.331–c.387
SAINT MONICA'S LIFE

387
CONVERSION OF SAINT AUGUSTINE

c.400
CHRISTIANITY NAMED OFFICIAL
RELIGION OF THE ROMAN EMPIRE

410
ALARIC AND THE VISIGOTHS SACK ROME

The **Many** Meanings of **Church**

A Jesuit theologian, Avery Dulles, attended the Second Vatican Council and noticed that "church" has different meanings for different people. For some people the Church is primarily an institution. For others it is a community, or sacrament, or the messenger of the gospel, or the servant of those who are in need, or a form of discipleship. Father Dulles thought about these different meanings. He concluded that all of them are true, but each of them is less true without the others.

The Church as Institution:
The Church is an organization with a *hierarchy,* or structure of leadership. Like any institution, it defines its members according to specific rules. One must be baptized. One must respect the Church's teaching authority to remain in communion. The structure and laws governing the institution have helped keep the Church alive through twenty centuries. The Creed, the sacraments, and the liturgical practices of the Church are examples of how the Church functions as an institution.

The Church as Community: The Church is a community of believers. We gather at Mass because we believe in one God, follow one Lord, and are guided by one Spirit. We celebrate our common faith in the Eucharist and in the other sacraments. This idea of Church focuses more on the people of faith, their spirituality, and their connectedness, and less on the structures that surround and support them.

The Church as Sacrament: Though the Church is not one of the seven sacraments, Father Dulles used the term *sacrament* to point out that, as with the seven sacraments, Christ becomes present through the actions of the Church. A sacrament makes Christ's saving action real to us, much like the purpose of the Church.

The Church as Herald: In this model, the mission of the Church is to proclaim the kingdom of God, especially as it is presented in the Bible. The Dominicans were founded with the mission to preach the good news. In fact, their official title is "Order of Preachers." For the Dominicans, and for many others, this is the most important model of the Church.

The Church as Servant: As servant, the Church works together with other groups for the betterment of the human community. This model has many expressions, from working to change social structures to doing works of charity. Mother Teresa was a strong supporter of this model.

The Church as Disciple: We are all disciples of Christ. The more we choose to follow his life and teachings, the more virtuous our lives become. Together we are encouraged to live virtuously in the face of a society that often sends the message that selfish or dangerous actions are acceptable. As a community of disciples, we are called to live as Jesus did, and to help guide and support one another.

All of these models of the Church are true, and though each person has an opinion about which is most important, they are meant to be seen as a whole. The Church is fully alive in us when we join with the whole Church as a community of believers who seek God, experience Christ through our actions, listen to God's word, serve him by serving one another, and live as disciples of his Son.

Opening the Word

Dedication of the Lateran Basilica

For we are God's servants, working together; you are God's field, God's building. 1 Corinthians 3:9

Read *1 Corinthians 3* as well as *Matthew 28:18–20, Mark 16:15,* and *Acts 4:32–35.* What models of the Church are emphasized in each of the passages? How do we live these models today?

_____

_____

_____

_____

The Universal **Family**

Your school is more than a building with students, teachers, and a principal. Your school is the customs and traditions that make up its history. It's all the students who ever went there, and all the parents and teachers of the students. It's the after-school activities and the social events and the sports. There's even a school spirit that will be a part of who you are long after you graduate.

In the same way, the Church is more than the place we worship on Sunday and more than the priests and bishops. The Church is the body of all baptized people across the world and throughout time. The customs and traditions of the Church shape who we are and what we believe. The Church is alive because we, as members, take the Church wherever we go.

Early in our history the Church was called *catholic,* a word that means "universal." Later it was called *Roman Catholic* because Rome is the place where the apostles were martyred and the place from which the pope still leads the Church.

The Church is many things to many people, but it is at the same time larger and smaller than any one definition. It is larger because the Church is universal. But it is smaller because the Church is present in each of us. Through our relationships and actions, we represent Christ to others. So as a member of the Body of Christ, celebrate the institution, join with your community, experience the sacrament, share the gospel, serve others, and become a disciple.

Reflect on our call to bring Christ to the world. Share your responses and thoughts with your Faith Partner.

Faith Partnership

WRAP UP

- The Church is catholic, which means "universal."
- We experience the Church in our parishes and our families.
- The activity of the Church is the living expression of Christ in the world.
- The Church is fully alive in us when we join with the whole Church in all of its forms.

What questions do you have about the material in this chapter?

_____

_____

_____

Around the Group

Discuss the following questions as a group.

What are some ways that we live the models of the Church? What are some other models we can use to describe the Church?

After everyone has had a chance to share his or her responses, create a poster based on your new models.

_____

_____

_____

_____

What personal observations do you have about the group discussion and answer?

_____

_____

_____

_____

Briefly...

At the beginning of the chapter, you were asked to consider certain statements about you and the Church. Based on what you have learned about the Church, would you now change any of your answers? If so, which ones? Why?

_____

_____

_____

Choosing Good Friends

Expressions of Faith-

Our Church is a community of believers. We respect one another, we contribute to the well-being of each member, and we are at peace with each other and the world around us. Often the friends we choose uphold and support these values, but sometimes they don't. Choosing Good Friends is a skill that helps us live the Christian life we receive from our families and our parish.

Think About It-

Fill in the following categories of friends.

- Old friends I still have: _____
_____

- Old friends I wish I still had: _____
_____

- Friends who are younger: _____
_____

- Friends who are older: _____
_____

- Friends of the same gender: _____
_____

- Friends of the other gender: _____
_____

- People with whom I'd like to become friends:
_____
_____

Skill Steps-

Your friends influence you greatly, so it is very important to choose good friends. The skill of Choosing Good Friends can affect your spiritual health and happiness.

● I once was in a friendship that wasn't good because

_____

_____

● You can tell you are in a friendship that isn't good when

_____

_____

● List five things to look for when choosing good friends.

_____

_____

● List three things to beware of when choosing friends.

_____

_____

Check It Out-

Rate yourself on a scale of 1 to 5, with 1 being "almost never" and 5 being "almost always."

	1	2	3	4	5
Whatever I do, I try to do joyfully.	○	○	○	○	○
I try to live in peace with everyone.	○	○	○	○	○
I do my best to be patient with others.	○	○	○	○	○
I like to be generous with others.	○	○	○	○	○
I practice being faithful to my values.	○	○	○	○	○
Controlling myself isn't always easy, but I try.	○	○	○	○	○

Based on your ratings, what overall grade would you give yourself as a friend? _____

Closing Prayer-

Lord Jesus, you are always the best friend we have. You constantly share your life and your presence with us through our family and our friends. Help us always grow together in love with those you give us. Amen.

The Church in the World

Jesus, you showed us how to live a life of self-giving and generous love. Help us speak the truth and serve one another. Make us especially mindful of those most in need. Amen.

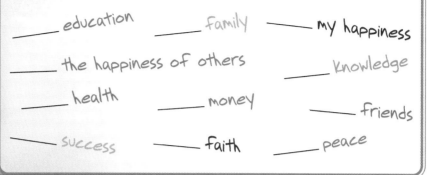

Rank the following items in order of importance to you:

_____ education   _____ family   _____ my happiness

_____ the happiness of others   _____ knowledge

_____ health   _____ money   _____ friends

_____ success   _____ faith   _____ peace

For the
Good of All

Many people calculate the wealth of this country in terms of how much money we have. But we are wealthy in other ways, too. We live in a society that provides social and educational opportunities. We can speak our opinions freely. Most of us can choose where we will live, what work we will do, and who our companions will be. Our government guarantees us "life, liberty, and the pursuit of happiness."

No matter how we define wealth, as Christians, we shouldn't cling to it selfishly. Jesus taught us how to live generously. He shared his wisdom and power with those who came to him in need. Jesus shared the wealth of God's love with us, keeping nothing for himself, not even his own life. As Mohandas Gandhi said, "There is enough in this world for everyone's need, but not for everyone's greed."

Neighbors in Need

Think of a time when you were lonely. Think of a time when you felt that someone hated you or when you felt discriminated against because of your race, gender, or family background.

When someone asked Jesus, "Who is my neighbor?" Jesus told him the parable of the Good Samaritan, which redefines the word *neighbor* for us. Jesus says that we are neighbors to others when we help them. And in a world  where inequality is common, someone always needs us. (See *Luke 10:29–37*.)

For a variety of reasons, many people do not have the basic necessities for life. Sometimes government leaders make dishonest or unwise decisions that result in poverty for their people. Wars destroy people's homes and their ability to make a living. Prejudice and discrimination often cause one group of people to act unjustly toward another. Still other suffering is caused by indifference.

People don't always stop to think that the products they buy might have been created at the expense of those who are poor. Rich nations sometimes ignore how their decisions affect developing nations. Harm to the natural environment negatively affects those who are poor more than it touches those who are well-to-do. Add to this natural disasters such as floods or drought, which cause enormous losses for large numbers of people, and you can see why Jesus said, "you always have the poor with you" *(Mark 14:7)*.

Focus On

Theological Virtues
The three theological virtues of faith, hope, and love support us in our effort to act in ways that show that all people are children of God.

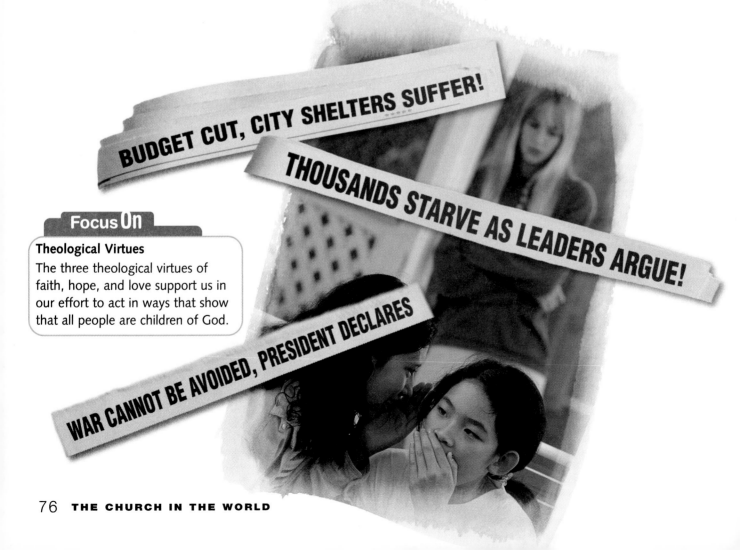

BUDGET CUT, CITY SHELTERS SUFFER!

THOUSANDS STARVE AS LEADERS ARGUE!

WAR CANNOT BE AVOIDED, PRESIDENT DECLARES

What to Do?

We have been looking at how the Church is "one, holy, Catholic, and apostolic." In an earlier chapter we read that the word *apostolic* describes how the Church is founded on the work of the apostles. Another word that comes from the same root is *apostolate,* which means "sent out" into the world. All who are baptized share in the apostolate of the Church, to announce the good news and help others as Jesus taught us.

When we look at the many causes of world suffering, we may become discouraged. What can we do? When we think of acting charitably toward those in need, we may imagine a generous person handing a coin to a beggar. But that is not the definition of Christian charity. **Charity,** one of the *theological virtues,* is another word for love. True charity is what the children of God, equal in God's eyes, share with one another.

Each of us has been invited to participate in the story of God's love and generosity. When we share what we have with people in need, we are sharing what is a gift from God and what he intends for us to share. **Social justice** requires that we give to our neighbor what is rightfully due to him or her. The Church teaches that social justice means respect for the human person, equality, and *solidarity,* or working together. When we respect the human person, we recognize that everyone has a right to live with dignity. We should treat each person as we would expect to be treated. Honoring social justice also means that we treat one another equally. We should honor our differences in gender, culture, and race, but we have a right to expect equal treatment, nonetheless. Through solidarity, in fact, we can work to make sure we are being treated both respectfully and equally. Through the Christian virtue of solidarity, we share material and spiritual goods selflessly.

He has told you, O mortal, what is good; and what does the LORD require of you but to do justice, and to love kindness, and to walk humbly with your God? Micah 6:8

List the first three actions that come to your mind for each of the three things the Lord requires of you.

Do Justice	Love Kindness	Walk Humbly with God

Faith and **Works**

CORPORAL WORKS OF MERCY

- Feed the hungry
- Give drink to the thirsty
- Bury the dead
- Visit the sick
- Shelter the homeless
- Visit the imprisoned
- Clothe the naked

We often see people who claim to be faithful, but whose actions are anything but. The author of the Letter of James was faced with this kind of people, so he gave them a wake-up call. "What good is it, my brothers and sisters," he wrote, "if you say you have faith but do not have works? Can faith save you? If a brother or sister is naked and lacks daily food, and one of you says to them, 'Go in peace; keep warm and eat your fill,' and yet you do not supply their bodily needs, what is the good of that? So faith by itself, if it has no works, is dead" (*James 2:14–17*).

In the same way, we cannot call ourselves the Church unless we act like the Body of Christ in the world. Like Jesus, we work for the **common good,** performing works that benefit the entire community. We must consider how our actions affect the needs and rights of others before we act. The common good is negatively affected when we buy clothes or toys made in *sweatshops,* where

OUR CHRISTIAN JOURNEY

Economic Justice for All The history of our country has been marked by the full participation of its members in shaping our common life. In 1986 the U.S. Catholic Bishops called for "a new American experiment." The bishops argued that the same bold spirit used in democracy should be used for justice's sake. Decisions concerning employment, poverty, agriculture, and the global economy should be made with an eye to economic justice. The bishops' pastoral letter, *Economic Justice for All,* affirms the teachings of the Second Vatican Council that the human person is "the source, the center, and the purpose of all socio-economic life."

For more information: Find a copy of the 1998 U.S. Catholic Bishops' *Sharing Catholic Social Teaching.* What are several of the key themes that are at the heart of our Catholic social tradition?

1850   **2000**

1891
ENCYCLICAL *ON THE CONDITION OF WORKING PEOPLE* ISSUED BY POPE LEO XIII

1965
PASTORAL LETTER *CONSTITUTION ON THE CHURCH IN THE MODERN WORLD* ISSUED

1986
U.S. CATHOLIC BISHOPS PUBLISH *ECONOMIC JUSTICE FOR ALL*

1998
U.S. CATHOLIC BISHOPS PUBLISH *SHARING CATHOLIC SOCIAL TEACHING*

those who are poor—often women and children—are overworked and underpaid to keep production costs down. The common good is damaged when migrant farmworkers are not given adequate protection from the hazardous chemicals used on crops. Even when the majority benefits from something that hurts a minority, the cost is too high.

We learn to recognize that sometimes protecting the common good means buying a generic pair of jeans made in a humane factory rather than a popular brand that we know was made by sweatshop labor. Or it can mean *boycotting* a particular kind of fruit or vegetable until the conditions of the farmworkers improve. It may also mean recycling, even though we find it inconvenient, to preserve clean air, water, or other resources.

The **Way** of **Compassion**

Compassion literally means that we "suffer with" others. The point is not to have everyone suffering, but to share burdens. We can learn compassion by doing **works of mercy,** actions modeled on the life of Jesus. The Church's list of works of mercy gives us concrete ways to work for justice, peace, and love in our community. The Corporal Works of Mercy are examples of caring for the material needs of others. The Spiritual Works of Mercy are actions we take to care for others' spiritual needs, which are more difficult to see. (See the charts on these pages to review the Corporal and Spiritual Works of Mercy.) When we practice the Works of Mercy, we truly participate in the apostolate of the Church.

With your Faith Partner, share a time when you received or did a work of mercy.

SPIRITUAL WORKS OF MERCY

- Warn the sinner
- Forgive injuries
- Counsel the doubtful
- Bear wrongs patiently
- Teach the ignorant
- Pray for the living and the dead
- Comfort the sorrowful

Sharing the World

Imagine what life would be like if there were no sharing. How would you have survived if your family hadn't shared their food with you when you were little? How much fun would you have if your friends never shared their time with you? Where would you go if nobody shared the roads or the sidewalks? What would school be like if teachers refused to share what they know with their students?

Each of us has wealth that we can share with others. That doesn't mean that we have a lot of money. It means that we have God-given talents and gifts that we can share with one another. Some of us may be good at playing the piano. With this talent, we might volunteer to share the gift of music with people in care centers or teach a child how to play. If we are good at building things, we can offer our services to people with low incomes who need help with home repairs. And each of us, regardless of our physical skills, can share the gift of conversation and friendship with those who need it.

The work of the Church is to bring the saving mission of Jesus Christ into the world. When we share our time, our energy, our money, and our abilities, we are serving Christ himself. Together, we strive for justice and peace in our community and in our world.

Reflect on how you and your friends can work for justice, peace, and the common good. Share your thoughts with your Faith Partner.

FaiTH PaRTNeRShip

WRAP UP

- Jesus taught us by example to serve others, regardless of education, race, gender, or background, because each person is a child of God.

- We can work for justice and live charitably by giving people what is their due and by sharing what we have with those in need.

- The apostolate of the Church is to announce the good news and help others as Jesus taught us.

- When we work for the common good, we consider the needs and rights of others before we act.

- The Corporal and Spiritual Works of Mercy are ways to model our life on the actions of Jesus.

Write some questions you have about the material in this chapter.

_____

_____

_____

Around the Group

Discuss the following question as a group.

Which of the Corporal Works of Mercy do you find easiest to practice?

After everyone has had a chance to share his or her responses, come up with a group answer upon which everyone can agree.

_____

_____

_____

_____

What personal observations do you have about the group discussion and answer?

_____

_____

_____

_____

Briefly...

At the beginning of the chapter, you ranked items in your life in order of importance. Based on what you have learned in the chapter, what would you rank differently?

_____

_____

_____

_____

Choosing Good Friends

Expressions of Faith—

Jesus taught us that to be friends we need to be merciful and charitable. The skill of Choosing Good Friends helps us surround ourselves with others who can help us and support our decisions.

Skill Steps—

It is important to make good choices about who our friends are.

Here are some key points to remember:

- A daily goal for us is to love others.
- Being generous is a way we help our friends.
- We are called to live in peace with others.
- We are faithful friends when we do what's right.

Skill Builder—

When asked if it's important that a good friend be a person of character, a student told his teacher, "Not really. My best friend is untruthful. I don't believe a word he tells me. He never tells the complete truth. He never admits to anything he does wrong. But he's my best friend because he is loyal. He will help me out every time I need him. My dad died when I was young, and my friend has stuck by me closer than a brother."

○ What is the difference between a loyal friend and a friend who is good?

_____

_____

○ What would someone be like who is both a loyal friend and a friend who is good?

_____

_____

Share your responses and thoughts with your Faith Partner.

Putting It into Practice-

○ Make a list of things to keep in mind when choosing good (virtuous) friends:

_____

_____

_____

○ The Bible contains many wise sayings, or proverbs, about friends who are good. Look up some of the following passages in your Bible: *Proverbs 11:13, Proverbs 17:9, Proverbs 17:17, Proverbs 18:24, Proverbs 19:6, Ephesians 4:25, 1 Peter 3:8.*

Compose your own proverb about the importance of choosing a friend who is good.

_____

_____

_____

_____

_____

Compose your own proverb about the best way to choose a friend who is good.

_____

_____

_____

_____

_____

Closing Prayer-

Dear Jesus, you have called us your friends and invited us to be the community of friends who make up the Church. May we always imitate you through our works of charity, for you are the way that leads to eternal joy. Amen.

CHAPTER 9

Now
and Forever

God of all ages, you are without beginning and without end. Thank you for Jesus, your Son, who, through his time on earth, has given us a glimpse of your kingdom. Help us learn from his life so that we might one day be with you in heaven. Amen.

Complete the statements on the lines provided.

Heaven is _____

_____

Hell is _____

_____

To go to heaven I must _____

_____

Conversion

Judging others is all too easy. A bad first impression of someone can prevent our learning any more about that person, and we may assume that he or she will never change. But Jesus warned us about judging others. We are often wrong and only God sees what is in the human heart.

With God's help, people can change for the better. Everyone, regardless of what each has done or failed to do, can turn away from sin and turn back to God. No matter how much our lives may be affected by sinful attitudes and actions, no one is beyond God's grace.

Every new day brings with it the hope of new beginnings. As long as we live, there are new opportunities to make good choices. God gives us the gift of today to open our hearts to love. Tomorrow is an unopened book.

Looking for Happiness

If you listed all the things that make you happy, your list might include special people, a perfect touchdown, an excellent movie, or a sunny beach on a summer day. What makes someone happy is something each person answers for himself or herself. But the desire for happiness is universal.

Our faith teaches us that God alone is the source of happiness. Faith guarantees us what the world cannot give: happiness, now and forever.

The state of eternal joy that God promises us is known as beatitude, or "blessedness." When we hear the word **Beatitudes,** we think of Jesus' Sermon on the Mount. (See *Matthew 5:3–12.*) In this sermon Jesus taught his disciples to think about happiness in a new

way. In the Beatitudes Jesus taught that blessedness, or true happiness, is promised to those who are poor, sad, humble, and persecuted for the sake of justice. We probably would not include these people in the list of those who are happy, yet Jesus does.

With the Beatitudes Jesus told us how to live in the kingdom of God on earth and how we will be rewarded for doing so. The **kingdom of God** is God's reign of justice, love, and peace. God's kingdom is far different from the kingdoms and governments of earth, in which happiness seems tied to money, power, and prestige. The Beatitudes and the parables of Jesus tell us that in the kingdom of God, "the last will be first, and the first will be last" *(Matthew 20:16).*

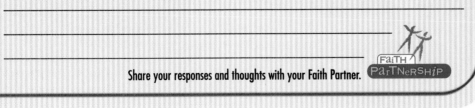

Catholics Believe

Beatitude makes us sharers in the nature of God and in eternal life. See Catechism, #1721.

Brainstorm three ways you can be a blessing to those who are hurting among your friends, peers, and family.

_____

_____

_____

Share your responses and thoughts with your Faith Partner.

Now and Later

We live in the kingdom of God, proclaimed and brought about by Jesus. But when we pray, "Thy kingdom come," we are praying for the fullness of God's kingdom at the end of time. We are told that when the day of final judgment arrives, those who are virtuous will reign forever with Christ and the universe will be renewed. We will experience a "new heaven" and a "new earth," and God's plan will finally be realized. When creation passes away, the kingdom of God will be fully present, and God will be "all in all." (See *1 Corinthians 15:28.*) When we talk about what will happen at the end of time, we are talking about the *eschaton,* or "the last things." The study of the end times is called **eschatology.**

Until the time of Jesus' return, though, we must continue to work for justice and peace. Jesus told us that we can experience God's kingdom in small ways in our daily lives, and so we should. (See *Luke 17:20–21.*) Every act of justice we participate in, every time we share our love with others, and every decision we make for peace is a sign of God's kingdom. And each act will be important when Christ returns in glory.

Opening the Word

2nd Sunday of Advent, Cycle B

[I]n accordance with his promise, we wait for new heavens and a new earth, where righteousness is at home. 2 Peter 3:13

Read *2 Peter 3:8–13* as well as *John 5:25–29* and *Revelation 21:1–5.* Based on these readings, make a slogan to post at home.

Images of Hell Hell has always had a hold on artists' imaginations. In Scripture it is symbolically described as a state of torment and flame. The fourteenth-century writer Dante Alighieri described hell in his *Inferno* as a cold, dark place removed from the warmth and light of God. In the nineteenth century sculptor Auguste Rodin, inspired by Dante, created his *Gates of Hell,* a bronze work intended to cover the doors of a French museum that was never completed. Although images of hell capture our imagination, the Church today describes hell simply as the eternal separation from God.

For more information: Research the artist's vision of hell in Dante's *Inferno* or books of Christian art at your library.

The Role of
the Church

Jesus shows us his Father in his teachings, his power over sin and death, and his great love for us. When the disciple Philip asked Jesus to show him the Father, Jesus told Philip that he didn't have to see the Father. To see Jesus was to see the Father. (See *John 14:8–9.*) In this sense, Jesus is the sacrament of God. Because of the incarnation and redemption, Jesus is the sacrament of salvation, the way in which salvation comes to us from God.

Just as Jesus is the sacrament of God and salvation, the Church is the sacrament of Jesus. The Church is a sign of our relationship with God and the unity of all humanity. It is a sign of salvation in Jesus. Wherever the Church acts for justice, love, and peace, people see Jesus. As the Church spreads the gospel, Jesus is present. Through the sacraments the Church welcomes, forgives, reconciles, and heals in the name of Jesus who saves. Christ dwells on earth in his Church, and the kingdom of God proclaimed by the Church will come to its fullness when Christ returns in glory.

The End of Time

The greatest decision we'll ever make is in regard to what happens to us when we die. It's a choice we make in everything we do. When we choose to be loving or unloving, our choice affects our destiny.

Heaven is the perfect and final completion of our life with God. If we are with God throughout our lives, it will be no surprise to us to be with him in eternity. **Hell** is eternal separation from God. If we reject God's love and mercy during our lives and at the moment of our death, complete separation from God is what we will have chosen.

Some of those who die have been friends of God, but have not achieved the closeness they might have had. The Church teaches that **purgatory** is the in-between state of *purification* between death and heaven for those whose love is not perfect.

The Church teaches that we will receive a **particular judgment** at the time of our death, when we will be judged according to our works and faith. Scripture also presents us with the image of a final judgment. The **last judgment** is the event at the end of time when we will see the results of our sins to the furthest consequence. If you want to know which actions Jesus is likely to question us about, read Jesus' teaching on the final judgment in *Matthew 25:31–46.*

The idea of a final judgment and hell may seem frightening to us, but we have no need to be afraid. Jesus greeted his disciples many times with the words, "Be not afraid!" We can choose heaven right now by choosing a life of love.

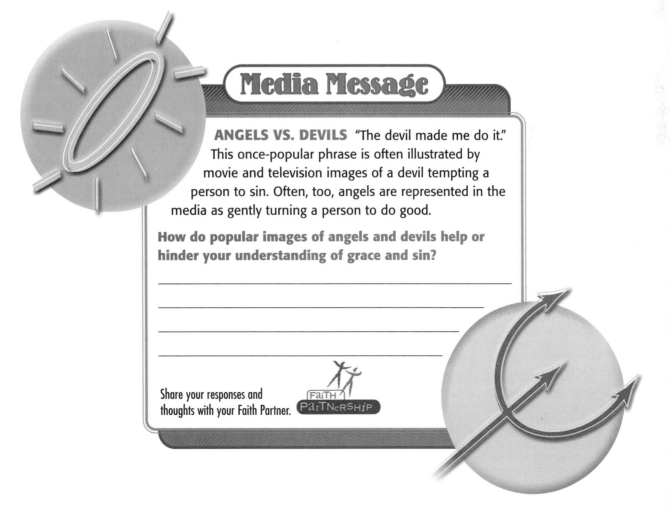

Media Message

ANGELS VS. DEVILS "The devil made me do it." This once-popular phrase is often illustrated by movie and television images of a devil tempting a person to sin. Often, too, angels are represented in the media as gently turning a person to do good.

How do popular images of angels and devils help or hinder your understanding of grace and sin?

_____

_____

_____

_____

Share your responses and thoughts with your Faith Partner.

FAITH PARTNERSHIP

Forever **Blessed**

What if the world as we know it got turned around? What if those who are poor suddenly had more than those who are rich? What if the school football team's worst player grew up to become the Super Bowl MVP and the star quarterback wouldn't even be a starter on his college team?

Jesus taught that the kingdom of God is like that: the last will be first and the first will be last. Those who are poor, hungry, sad, or persecuted are blessed. True happiness belongs to those who least expect to find it in this world.

We can participate in the reality of God's kingdom now. We experience the kingdom when we live the Beatitudes. Look for opportunities to help those in need. Together with your friends, organize a service project or talk with your local parish about assisting with projects that have already been created. Meet with other faith communities in your area to discover how they work to help others.

We don't expect to live in this world forever. This world will pass away, but God's kingdom will come in its fullness and last forever. If Jesus were to ask you tomorrow what you have done to help those in need, what would you say?

Reflect on how you can live as Jesus taught. Share your thoughts with your Faith Partner.

WRAP UP

• We are called by God to be happy, both now in this world and forever in heaven.

• The Church is the sacrament of Christ and a sacrament of salvation.

• By living according to the teachings of Jesus, we participate in God's kingdom now.

• The least blessed of the world are the most blessed in the kingdom of God.

• At the end of our lives, we are judged by our faith and our actions. Our eternity is decided by the choices we have made in this world up to and including the end of our lives.

What questions do you have about the material you studied in this chapter?

_____

_____

_____

Around the Group

Discuss the following question as a group.

Which of the Beatitudes from the Sermon on the Mount *(Matthew 5:3–12)* best describes someone your age who is a follower of Jesus?

After everyone has had a chance to share his or her responses, come up with a group answer upon which everyone can agree.

_____

_____

_____

What personal observations do you have about the group discussion and answer?

_____

_____

_____

Briefly...

At the beginning of this chapter, you were asked what you must do to go to heaven. Practicing the works of mercy can help you prepare for heaven. What works of mercy are you most likely to practice? With which do you need help and why?

_____

_____

_____

_____

Practicing Empathy

Expressions of Faith

Jesus taught us to love each other in the same way that God loves us. This means we must practice empathy. Empathy is being aware of and sensitive to the thoughts, feelings, needs, and experiences of others. To love one another and work toward the common good, we need to practice empathy.

Scripture

[I]f anyone has caused pain . . . you should forgive and console him, so that he may not be overwhelmed by excessive sorrow. . . . I urge you to reaffirm your love for him.
2 Corinthians 2:5, 7–8

Think About It

Jesus practiced empathy and set an example for his disciples. In *John 8:2–11* a woman is accused of a crime and brought to Jesus for judgment. Jesus is aware of the trouble she faces and pardons her. In *John 5:1–9* Jesus encounters a paralyzed man who cannot help himself. Jesus understands the man's situation and heals him.

Consider this: **Your friend wears new clothes to school. At lunch someone accidentally spills ketchup on your friend's shirt.**

How would you feel in this situation?

_____

_____

How do you think your friend feels?

_____

_____

Now consider this: **Your class is taking a test, and the teacher thinks your best friend is looking at someone else's paper. The teacher sends your friend to the principal's office.**

How would you feel in this situation?

_____

_____

How do you think your friend feels?

_____

_____

Skill Steps-

In the previous examples you practice empathy by recognizing what *your friends* are feeling and understanding their reactions. You then respond in caring and helpful ways. Empathy leads to a Christian response you make to another person in need.

Consider the following situations and complete the sentences.

● Jenny's parents are going through a divorce.

I think Jenny feels _____

And I should _____

● Erin scored the winning goal in the soccer game.

I think Erin feels _____

And I should _____

● Your older brother's girlfriend just broke up with him.

I think he feels _____

And I should _____

● One of Eduardo's friends is being bullied.

I think Eduardo feels _____

And I should _____

Check It Out-

Place a check mark next to the sentences that apply to you.

○ I can sense what a person is feeling in most situations.

○ When I see someone in a difficult situation, I first react to what is happening and then I respond to the person's needs.

○ I find it difficult to know how to respond to someone else's needs.

Using a scale from 1 to 5 (with 1 the lowest and 5 the highest), how would you rate your ability to show empathy to your friends? _____

To strangers? _____ To those whom you dislike? _____

Closing Prayer-

O God, teach us to love others the way you love us. May we be compassionate as you are compassionate. Amen.

Sharing
Our Faith

God of truth, you sent your Son to be the word made flesh, and the way for us to follow. Strengthen us for the mission of your Church so that your word may go out to all the world. Amen.

Read through the reflection below and circle any phrases that answer the question for you.

How do you show others that you believe in Jesus Christ?

wear religious clothing or jewelry   go to church

        the way I behave   have a cross in my room

things I say

        movies I watch   my values   music I listen to

praying at meals   avoid stereotyping and put-downs

What do you think is the most effective way to witness to your Christian faith?

_____

_____

_____

_____

Me, an Evangelist?

Have you ever seen people on television preaching about Jesus? Or perhaps you've answered the door at home and found a stranger standing there, asking whether you've been saved. These people are the ones we normally think of as evangelists. Like the four evangelists of the Bible—Matthew, Mark, Luke, and John—today's evangelists feel called to spread the gospel.

Words are important. They are our primary way of communicating how we feel and what we think. In the work of evangelization, words help us explain to others what we believe and what our faith means to us. But we all know that words do not tell the whole story. As Saint James wrote, faith without works is dead. (See *James 2:17.*) If our actions are not in agreement with our words, people will not believe.

Getting the
Word Out

In 1899 some Christian businessmen in Wisconsin dedicated themselves to making Scripture available to travelers. For more than a hundred years, the group, now known worldwide as Gideons International, has placed Bibles in hotels and motels free of charge, bringing God's word to people as they journey from place to place. The Gideons were prompted to this mission by the word of Jesus and the example of his followers.

After the resurrection Jesus commanded his followers to go and make disciples of all nations. (See *Matthew 28:19*.) The call to **evangelize,** or spread the good news, was central to the mission of the early Church, but there were no written Gospels for a generation or more after the ascension of Jesus. To spread the good news, the apostles moved from town to town, telling the story.

To strengthen and support the new faith in the communities he had evangelized, Saint Paul wrote letters to his converts. The letters of encouragement and instruction written by Paul and others became part of the New Testament. After Peter and Paul were martyred in Rome, several eyewitnesses to the life of Jesus recognized that it was time to write their memories of him. The four Gospels of the New Testament were written between A.D. 60 and A.D. 100.

But that didn't mean that people had Bibles. The invention of the printing press was still centuries away. For this reason, the Church couldn't use Bibles to spread the word. The main method of evangelization has always been through the words and actions of Jesus' disciples.

Opening the Word

14th Sunday of Ordinary Time, Cycle C

After this the Lord appointed seventy others and sent them on ahead of him in pairs to every town and place where he himself intended to go. Luke 10:1

Read *Luke 10:1–9* as well as *Acts 4:13–20* and *1 Corinthians 2:1–5*. What does it mean to evangelize?

_____

_____

Good News to **Share**

In the thirteenth century Dominic de Guzman founded a religious community called the Order of Preachers. Now known as the Dominicans, these priests, brothers, and sisters are dedicated to sharing the good news through preaching. But preaching is not the only way to spread the gospel. At the same time that Saint Dominic was starting his order, Saint Francis of Assisi was gathering his friends in Italy to share the task of evangelization. Francis believed that a life of poverty, chosen freely, was the best witness to God's love.

In time, other religious communities found ways to evangelize. The Salesians, founded by John Bosco in nineteenth-century Italy, evangelized youth by caring for their corporal and spiritual needs. The Sisters of Mercy in Ireland took care of women who were poor. The compassion demonstrated by these orders signaled the good news.

OUR CHRISTIAN JOURNEY

Through Care and Counsel John Bosco grew up fatherless and poor. Perhaps that's why he had a special love for youth in need of care and guidance. As a priest, he first evangelized boys by performing juggling acts in the street and gathering them to teach them about the Christian faith. To help make the boys employable, John taught them trades, such as shoemaking, tailoring, and printing. Soon, many of the boys he trained began helping him with his ministry. John became an expert on youth ministry and counseling. Later in his life John founded the Salesian Order of priests and brothers to carry out his work of housing young men and offering them job training and spiritual guidance. He also founded the Daughters of Our Lady, Help of Christians, to train and educate young women. His feast day is January 31.

For more information: Research the work of the Salesians (*www.salesians.org*) and Daughters of Our Lady, Help of Christians (*www.fmusa.org*) on the Internet or in a book on saints.

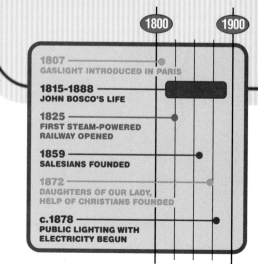

1800 **1900**

1807
GASLIGHT INTRODUCED IN PARIS

1815-1888
JOHN BOSCO'S LIFE

1825
FIRST STEAM-POWERED RAILWAY OPENED

1859
SALESIANS FOUNDED

1872
DAUGHTERS OF OUR LADY, HELP OF CHRISTIANS FOUNDED

c.1878
PUBLIC LIGHTING WITH ELECTRICITY BEGUN

Many Ways to Evangelize

As the Nicene Creed says, the Church is one, holy, catholic, and apostolic. These four **marks of the Church** reveal the presence of the Holy Spirit at work within us. To be apostolic means to share in the teaching and mission of the first apostles. Like Peter, Paul, James, and other leaders of the early Church, we have news too good to keep to ourselves. In fact, priests and deacons are ordained to proclaim the word. The Holy Spirit leads us in the many avenues of evangelization.

Catholic journalism is an avenue of evangelizing that serves tens of millions of people in our country alone. And, as Pope Paul VI once wrote, the Church must begin its evangelizing mission by being evangelized itself. Catholic newspapers, magazines, and other publications help us better understand our faith and the work of the Church.

The Paulist Fathers, an order of priests in the United States, was started by Isaac Hecker. Excited by the opportunities to evangelize

While the Salesians and Sisters of Mercy were beginning their work in Europe, the Sisters of Charity, led by a widow named Elizabeth Bayley Seton, began their service to people in the United States. The Sisters of Charity run schools, orphanages, and hospitals.

Some religious communities are considered missionaries because, through their words and work, they spread the gospel far and wide. The Maryknoll missionaries are one example of a missionary community. This community includes both lay people and men and women religious in its work. Through the works of charity of all communities, the good news of Jesus Christ is shared with others.

Our Global Community

Base Communities

In Brazil in 1956, some communities of believers who, because of their remote location, were without a priest, began to gather for Sunday service. These base communities were generally led by lay people who gathered the faithful together to read and reflect on Scripture. They applied the readings to their daily lives and committed themselves to personal conversion and social change in light of the gospel. If the Eucharist was reserved in their Church, they would share Communion. Today base communities continue to thrive in Latin America, Africa, Asia, and North America.

Reflect on what it might be like to belong to a base community. Share your thoughts with your Faith Partner.

through modern media, he began his work by shouting through a megaphone from a moving vehicle. Following the example of Saint Paul, he traveled from town to town holding *revivals*. Eventually, the Paulists began a publishing company; today they also produce radio programs, television spots, and videos. They also staff many Newman Centers for Catholic college students attending public universities.

Not only does the Church spread the gospel message verbally, it also does works of charity and justice. The Campaign for Human Development was started by the U.S. Catholic bishops in 1969. This organization educates people about poverty and its causes. It also provides money for programs that take direct action to counteract poverty. Programs that qualify for help from the campaign assist those who are poor in improving their circumstances for the long term.

Another organization, Catholic Charities, operates in every diocese in the United States, serving the needs of people who are poor and providing a variety of social services. Some of these services include counseling and adoption programs.

Catholic Relief Services goes around the world to assist people suffering from natural disasters and war. The Catholic Worker is a lay apostolate that operates houses of hospitality in many cities. Catholic Worker communities have two goals: to meet the immediate needs of those who are poor and to speak out against the injustices that cause poverty.

Through both word and deed, the evangelizing mission of the Catholic Church is alive and well.

Catholics Believe

God desires the salvation of all people. The Church must be missionary so that all people can come to know the truth and thus find salvation. See Catechism, #851.

If you were a modern missionary in your community, what methods would you use to spread the gospel message?

_____

_____

_____

Spreading the **Word**

From its beginning the Church has been filled with the desire to spread the good news of Jesus Christ. Today we are the missionaries whom Jesus calls to be witnesses of gospel joy. The Holy Spirit empowers us to live Christian lives and preach the gospel as did the apostles, saints, and missionaries of history. We put our faith into practice so that others can see the fruitfulness of our lives and come to know Christ as we do.

With the power and guidance of the Holy Spirit, we can dedicate our lives to service of others. And through our example, others will be drawn to Christ. Often the people we think live the most perfect lives of service are ordained or members of a religious community. Though we should always consider religious life as a possible vocation, each of us has the same opportunities to spread the word as priests, deacons, and men and women religious. We can become readers at Mass, help teach religious education to those who are younger, or simply spread the gospel message through our everyday words and actions.

There are as many ways to share our faith with others as we can imagine. When we open our lives to God and our hearts to those around us, we become examples of the Christian way of life. We represent the love of Jesus.

Reflect on the people around you who are models for evangelization, especially those who evangelize youth. Share your thoughts with your Faith Partner.

WRAP UP

- Jesus sent the apostles out into the world to preach the gospel and teach the Christian way of life.

- The apostles spread the gospel to others through their words and their good deeds.

- By living according to the teaching of Jesus Christ, saints of every age have been powerful witnesses of gospel joy.

- Today the apostolic work of the Church continues through members who evangelize in word and deed.

- The Holy Spirit gives us power to live fruitful lives of service so that others will be drawn to Christ.

What questions do you have about the material in this chapter?

_____

_____

_____

Around the Group

Discuss the following question as a group.

What more could the Catholic Church be doing today to evangelize?

After everyone has had a chance to share his or her responses, come up with a group answer upon which everyone can agree.

_____

_____

_____

_____

What personal observations do you have about the group discussion and answer?

_____

_____

_____

_____

Briefly...

At the beginning of this chapter, you were asked to identify the most effective way to witness to your Christian faith, or evangelize. Who are the most powerful role models of evangelization in your life?

_____

_____

_____

SKILLS FOR Christian Living

Practicing Empathy

Expressions of Faith—

Looking back over history, you can see how the apostles and saints evangelized the world in which they lived through their teaching, preaching, and good works. Today we too are called to proclaim the good news of God's love by what we say and do. Practicing empathy is a way we can show our commitment to living as followers of Christ.

Scripture

For by grace you have been saved through faith, and this is not your own doing; it is the gift of God—not the result of works, so that no one may boast. For we are what he has made us, created in Christ Jesus for good works, which God prepared beforehand to be our way of life.

Ephesians 2:8–10 | 4th Sunday of Lent, Cycle B

Skill Steps—

Empathy is being aware of and being sensitive to the thoughts, feelings, needs, and experience of others.
Here are some key points to remember:

● One way of showing our Christian love is by practicing empathy.

● The skill of practicing empathy contains the two steps of recognizing the experiences of others and responding in a Christian way.

Skill Builder—

Recognize Respond

Write down what each different person is feeling and how you could respond in each of these situations:

○ Your mom has had to work more hours than usual. When she gets home she is so tired she often doesn't talk to anyone.

She is probably feeling _____

To help her, I can _____

○ A classmate never gets invited to be with your group of friends. At lunch you see this person sitting alone more and more frequently.

He or she is feeling _____

To help him or her, I can _____

○ Now finish the following sentence:

The last time I practiced empathy was when _____

_____

Putting It into Practice-

Keeping in mind the Scripture passage from *Ephesians 2:8–10,* think of two people you know who are going through hard times right now.

What do you think the first person is feeling? _____
_____
_____
_____

What should be your Christian response? _____
_____
_____
_____

What do you think the other person is feeling? _____
_____
_____
_____

What should be your Christian response? _____
_____
_____
_____

We can practice empathy in many aspects of our lives. We can practice it with people we know and people we have never met. Try to practice this skill with at least one person every day.

What is the most important thing you have learned about the skill of Practicing Empathy?

_____
_____
_____

Closing Prayer-

God our Creator, you call us to share your love in all we say and do. Help us live according to the teachings of your **Son,** Jesus Christ. Give us the power we need to be the living word of life and love for others. We ask this in **Jesus'** name. Amen.

Prayers and **Resources**

The Lord's Prayer

Our Father, who art in heaven,
hallowed be thy name;
thy kingdom come;
thy will be done on earth as it is in heaven.
Give us this day our daily bread;
and forgive us our trespasses
as we forgive those who trespass against us;
and lead us not into temptation,
but deliver us from evil.
Amen.

Hail Mary

Hail, Mary, full of grace,
the Lord is with you!
Blessed are you among women,
and blessed is the fruit of your womb, Jesus.
Holy Mary, Mother of God,
pray for us sinners,
now and at the hour of our death.
Amen.

THE TEN COMMANDMENTS

1. I am the Lord your God. You shall not have strange gods before me.

2. You shall not take the name of the Lord your God in vain.

3. Remember to keep holy the Lord's day.

4. Honor your father and your mother.

5. You shall not kill.

6. You shall not commit adultery.

7. You shall not steal.

8. You shall not bear false witness against your neighbor.

9. You shall not covet your neighbor's wife.

10. You shall not covet your neighbor's goods.

THE BEATITUDES

Blessed are the poor in spirit,
    for theirs is the kingdom
    of heaven.

Blessed are they who mourn,
    for they will be comforted.

Blessed are the meek,
    for they will inherit the land.

Blessed are they who hunger and
thirst for righteousness,
    for they will be satisfied.

Blessed are the merciful,
    for they will be shown mercy.

Blessed are the clean of heart,
    for they will see God.

Blessed are the peacemakers,
    for they will be called children
    of God.

Blessed are they who are persecuted
for the sake of righteousness,
    for theirs is the kingdom
    of heaven.
(Matthew 5:3–10)

Glory to the Father (Doxology)

Glory to the Father, and to the Son,
and to the Holy Spirit:
as it was in the beginning, is now,
and will be for ever.
Amen.

Gifts of the Holy Spirit

Wisdom
Understanding
Right judgment (Counsel)
Courage (Fortitude)
Knowledge
Reverence (Piety)
Wonder and awe (Fear of the Lord)

Fruits of the Spirit

Charity
Joy
Peace
Patience
Kindness
Goodness
Generosity
Gentleness
Faithfulness
Modesty
Self-control
Chastity

Act of Contrition

My God,
I am sorry for my sins with all my
heart.
In choosing to do wrong
and failing to do good,
I have sinned against you
whom I should love above all things.
I firmly intend, with your help,
to do penance,
to sin no more,
and to avoid whatever leads me to sin.
Our Savior Jesus Christ
suffered and died for us.
In his name, my God, have mercy.

Works of Mercy

Corporal (for the body)
Feed the hungry.
Give drink to the thirsty.
Clothe the naked.
Shelter the homeless.
Visit the sick.
Visit the imprisoned.
Bury the dead.

Spiritual (for the spirit)
Warn the sinner.
Teach the ignorant.
Counsel the doubtful.
Comfort the sorrowful.
Bear wrongs patiently.
Forgive injuries.
Pray for the living and the dead.

PRECEPTS OF THE CHURCH

1. Take part in the Mass on Sundays and holy days. Keep these days holy and avoid unnecessary work.

2. Celebrate the Sacrament of Reconciliation at least once a year if there is serious sin.

3. Receive Holy Communion at least once a year during Easter time.

4. Fast and abstain on days of penance.

5. Give your time, gifts, and money to support the Church.

The Apostles' Creed

I believe in God, the Father almighty,
  creator of heaven and earth.
I believe in Jesus Christ, his only Son,
  our Lord.
  He was conceived by the power of the
    Holy Spirit
    and born of the Virgin Mary.
  He suffered under Pontius Pilate,
    was crucified, died, and was buried.
  He descended to the dead.
  On the third day, he rose again.
He ascended into heaven,
  and is seated at the right hand
    of the Father.
  He will come again to judge the
    living and the dead.
I believe in the Holy Spirit,
  the holy catholic Church,
  the communion of saints,
  the forgiveness of sins,
  the resurrection of the body,
  and life everlasting. Amen.

The Nicene Creed

We believe in one God,
  the Father, the Almighty,
  maker of heaven and earth,
  of all that is, seen and unseen.
We believe in one Lord, Jesus Christ,
  the only Son of God,
  eternally begotten of the Father,
  God from God, Light from Light,
  true God from true God,
  begotten, not made, one in Being
    with the Father.
  Through him all things were made.
  For us men and for our salvation
    he came down from heaven:
  by the power of the Holy Spirit
    he was born of the Virgin Mary,
    and became man.
  For our sake he was crucified under
    Pontius Pilate;
  he suffered, died, and was buried.
  On the third day he rose again
    in fulfillment of the Scriptures;
he ascended into heaven
  and is seated at the right hand
    of the Father.
  He will come again in glory to judge
    the living and the dead,
    and his kingdom will have no end.
We believe in the Holy Spirit, the Lord,
  the giver of life,
  who proceeds from the Father and
    the Son.
  With the Father and the Son he is
    worshiped and glorified.
  He has spoken through the Prophets.
We believe in one holy catholic and
    apostolic Church.
We acknowledge one baptism for the
    forgiveness of sins.
We look for the resurrection
    of the dead,
    and the life of the world to come.
Amen.

The Liturgical Year

In the liturgical year the Church celebrates Jesus' life, death, resurrection, and ascension through its seasons and holy days. The liturgical year begins with the First Sunday of Advent.

The readings for the entire Church year are contained in the Lectionary. Readings for Sundays and solemnities of the Lord are placed in a three-year rotation—Cycle A, Cycle B, and Cycle C.

The Season of Advent begins in late November or early December. During Advent we recall the first coming of the Son of God into human history, and we prepare for the coming of Christ—in our hearts, in history, and at the end of time. The liturgical color for Advent is violet.

On Christmas we celebrate the Incarnation, the Son of God becoming one of us. The color for Christmas is white, a symbol of celebration and life in Christ. (Any time white is used, gold may be used.)

Lent is the season of prayer and sacrifice that begins with Ash Wednesday and lasts about forty days. Lent has always been a time of repentance through prayer, fasting, and almsgiving. The liturgical color for Lent is purple, a symbol of penance.

Easter is the high point of the liturgical year because it celebrates Jesus' resurrection from the dead. The week beginning with Palm Sunday is called Holy Week. Lent ends on Holy Thursday evening, when the Easter Triduum begins. The Triduum, or "three holy days," includes the observance of Holy Thursday, Good Friday, and the Easter Vigil on Holy Saturday. The liturgical color for the Easter Season is white, a symbol of our joy in experiencing new life in Christ. The Easter Season lasts about seven weeks (fifty days).

At Pentecost, we celebrate the gift of the Holy Spirit sent to the followers of Jesus gathered in the upper room in Jerusalem. The liturgical color for Pentecost is red, a symbol of the tongues as of fire on Pentecost and of how Christ and some of his followers (such as the early Christian martyrs) sacrificed their lives for love of God.

The majority of the liturgical year is called Ordinary Time, a time when the Church community reflects on what it means to walk in the footsteps of Jesus. The liturgical color for Ordinary Time is green, a symbol of hope and growth.

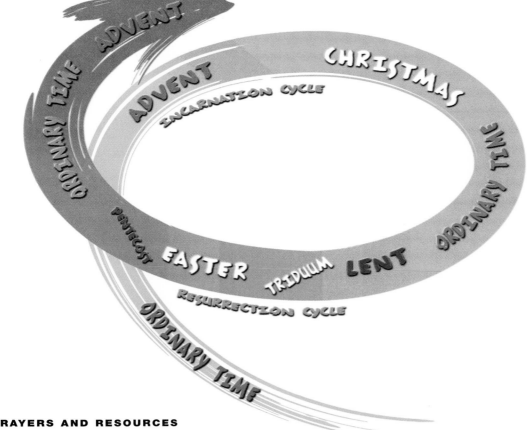

Glossary

A apostles — Twelve friends and followers of Jesus to whom he entrusted his mission. The number of apostles corresponds to the number of tribes of Israel.

Apostles' Creed — A formal statement based on the beliefs of the apostles.

apostolic — A description of the foundation and leadership, through the apostles, of Christ's Church.

B Beatitudes — Sayings of Jesus (*Matthew 5:3–10*) that sum up the way to live in God's kingdom and that point the way to true happiness. The word *beatitude* means "blessedness."

C catholic — Universal; the Church is catholic because its mission is to the whole world.

charity — Love for God and for our neighbor. Charity is a theological virtue and one of the fruits of the Holy Spirit.

Christ — A title for Jesus that means "anointed one."

common good — That which will benefit the entire community. As Christians we are called to perform works for the common good. Working for the common good means that we consider the needs and rights of others before we act.

communion of saints — All members of the Church, living and dead.

covenant — A sacred and binding promise or agreement joining God and humans in relationship. Jesus' sacrifice established the new and everlasting covenant, open to all who do God's will.

D disciple — A person who accepts, lives, and spreads the teachings of another.

domestic Church — The Church as it exists within the family.

E eschatology — The study of the end times.

evangelization — Giving witness to our faith by proclaiming the good news of Jesus Christ to the world through our words and actions.

G gospel — The good news of God's saving love. The first four books of the New Testament, which present Jesus' teachings, are called the Gospels.

H heaven — The perfect and final completion of human life in union with God.

hell — Eternal separation from God; the consequence of deliberately rejecting God's merciful love and forgiveness.

Holy Trinity — One God in three Persons—Father, Son, and Holy Spirit. The Trinity is the central mystery of the Catholic faith.

I infallibility — A charism given by Christ to the pope, and to the bishops in union with the pope, by which they speak without error on certain matters regarding faith and morals.

K kingdom of God — God's reign of justice, love, and peace. The kingdom of God is both present in our midst and yet to come in its fullness.

L last judgment — The event at the end of time when Jesus will judge the living and the dead based on their acceptance or refusal of grace and their works in Christ by means of faith.

liturgical year — The annual cycle of Church seasons and feasts that comprise the Church year. The liturgical year, which does not correspond to the traditional calendar, celebrates Christ's life, death, resurrection, and ascension.

Liturgy of the Eucharist — The term for the entire celebration of the Mass as well as for the specific part of the Mass that includes the Preparation of the Gifts, the Eucharistic Prayer, and Communion.

Liturgy of the Word — The first great part of the Mass, lasting from the first reading to the General Intercessions, that celebrates God's word.

M magisterium — The teaching authority of the Catholic Church, given by Christ through the Holy Spirit and found in the bishops in union with the pope.

marks of the Church — The identifying characteristics of the presence of the Holy Spirit in the Church. The Church is one, holy, catholic, and apostolic.

martyr — A saint or other holy person who witnessed to Christ and was killed because he or she was a follower of Jesus or because he or she upheld a Christian value.

N Nicene Creed — A statement of belief that expands on the Apostles' Creed and conveys our Christian beliefs.

P parable — A special kind of story used to teach. Parables were often used by Jesus to explain God's kingdom.

particular judgment — The event at the time of death at which a person is judged on his or her works and faith.

Paschal mystery — The saving mystery of Jesus' passion, death, resurrection, and ascension.

Pentateuch — The first five books of the Old Testament, also known as the Torah.

purgatory — The intermediate state of purification between death and heaven for those who die in God's friendship, but who are still imperfect.

R revelation — The process by which God makes himself known to us. The chief sources of revelation are God's creation, Scripture, salvation history, and Jesus (the fullness of revelation).

S sacrament — A celebration in which Jesus joins with the assembled community in liturgical actions that are efficacious signs and sources of God's grace.

salvation history — The story of God's loving actions on behalf of humans. Salvation history began with creation, continues through the events recorded in Scripture, and will last until the end of time.

sanctoral cycle — The feasts of the saints celebrated throughout the year.

Scripture — The word of God contained in the Bible. The word *scripture* means "holy writing."

social justice — Giving each person his or her due regardless of education, race, gender, or background because each person is a child of God.

W works of mercy — Actions modeled after the life of Jesus that show justice, love, and peace. The Corporal Works of Mercy are actions of care for the physical needs of others, while the Spiritual Works of Mercy are actions of care for the spiritual needs of others.